The Labor of God

The Labor of God

An Ignatian View of Church and Culture

Edited by William J. O'Brien

GEORGETOWN UNIVERSITY PRESS
Washington, D.C.

Library of Congress Cataloging-in-Publication Data

The labor of God : An Ignatian view of church and culture/ edited by
    William J. O'Brien
    ISBN 0-87840-527-5
        1. Ignatius, of Loyola, Saint, 1491-1556 2. Christianity and
    culture. 3. Latin America--History 4. Journalism, Religious.
    I. O'Brien, William James.
    BX4700.L7L29 1991
    261--dc20   91-24720

Contents

Preface

The community at Georgetown University is characterized by a shared set of moral commitments and a shared understanding of the nature of undergraduate education. Our shared moral commitments are shaped by the idea that a good centers each person's life and serves as a fundamental organizing principle. Georgetown wishes to ensure that during the course of their undergraduate years students are presented with this idea and given the opportunity to determine the good which will order and center their lives.

Georgetown University is built on a particular understanding of this good which is present in the life and work of two people: Jesus and Ignatius of Loyola. This good grounds the set of moral commitments which serve as a foundation for the Georgetown University community:

☐ *Belief in God and the spiritual life.* The Catholic vision, a sacramental vision, sees God in and through all things: in and through other people, events, places, and objects of this world. While this religious vision does not demand belief from the members of this community, all members are expected by virtue of their agreement to be members here, to respect the implications of this vision.

☐ *Human flourishing.* Human flourishing is an integration of the essential activities of play, learning, religion, friendship, aesthetic experience, knowledge, and practical reasonableness.[1] Such integration flows from a thoughtful, contemplative involvement in each of these activities.

☐ *Responsible citizenship.* Each member of the community has a responsibility to every other member. This responsibility extends beyond this campus to help others wherever we live and work. We have a particular commitment to help those in our communities who are in serious difficulty.

☐ *Free exchange of ideas.* The shaping of one's moral conscience requires that no inquiry be limited. The pathway to moral excellence is through the development of the intellect.

☐ *Diversity*. What we share as individuals is far greater than what divides us. We need to appreciate what we share in order to celebrate our diversity.

☐ *Love of truth*. To tell the truth, even when it is not popular or is painful in its consequences, is at the very base of our community as a university.

These moral commitments create an ethos or characteristic spirit for the university community. In addition to providing members of our community with a context within which to develop ethical responses to questions such as "Is this right or wrong?" and "Ought I to do this or that?" this ethos also creates a context in which to ask "How does this action square with the way I see myself in relation to this group?" or, collectively, "How will my actions affect the character of this group?"[2] Our students must wrestle with some very difficult questions:

☐ Where do I stand in relationship to my God?

☐ What is my responsibility to myself and what do I want to stand for in my life?

☐ What kind of person should I be?

☐ What types of responsibilities do I wish to undertake?

☐ What kinds of relationships do I wish to establish and under what conditions?

☐ What kind of family do I wish to raise and under what conditions?

☐ What are my obligations to my family, my community, my country, and my church, mosque or synagogue?

And, most importantly,

☐ What good will order my life and serve as a fundamental organizing principle?

In 1990-1991, the Office of Student Affairs sponsored a series of lectures that were intended to help clarify for this community the significance of our Jesuit tradition. The lectures were part of the celebration of the five hundredth anniversary of the birth of Ignatius Loyola and the four hundred fiftieth anniversary of the founding of the Society of Jesus. They offer an opportunity to reflect upon the shared commitment upon which our community is built. We present them with the hope that they will have as much meaning for members of other communities as they have for us.

John J. DeGioia
Dean of Student Affairs
June, 1991

Notes

[1] Cf. John Finnis, *Natural Law and Natural Rights* (Oxford: Clarendon Press, 1980), 86-90.

[2] I am indebted to Alan Mitchell, S.J., for his articulation of these questions.

Introduction

For Ignatius, founder of the Society of Jesus, "God is present in our lives, 'laboring for us' in all things; [God] can be discovered, through faith, in all natural and human events, in history as a whole, and most especially within the lived experience of each individual person."[1]

God labors for us in time; God is to be discovered in our lived experience.

The essays included in this volume were originally presented on the Georgetown University campus as a series of lectures on Jesuit education celebrating the five hundredth anniversary of the birth of Ignatius Loyola and the four hundred fiftieth anniversary of the founding of the Society of Jesus. Their authors look for the labor of God along academic corridors, in city libraries, amid moral dilemmas, in historical events, in personal lives, in journalism. The combined effect of their forays is to propel us into a similar survey of our life and times.

Leo J. O'Donovan, S.J., president of Georgetown University, opened the year-long celebration with the message that the university should be a place where faculty, students, administrators, and staff discern signs of the times by which they may be reliably guided. He believes that Ignatius Loyola, "master of discernment and choice," offers direction: discern where *life* is to be found, and choose life. In the midst of all the extraordinary events taking place in the last decade of the twentieth century, those of us who seek life can find an unmistakable sign of God's presence: the suffering love of the risen Christ encountered sacramentally in the Eucharist and personally in our own lived experience. As each of the later speakers elaborates on this most basic point of Ignatian spirituality, we cannot but become more deeply aware of the ultimate significance of decision points in our own lives and of our own need to discern well. From each we learn a bit more about how to go about that task.

Timothy Healy, S.J., president of the New York City Public Library and past president of Georgetown University, looks back on his years as a Jesuit and speaks of a deep dialectic in Jesuit life rooted in Ignatius's *Spiritual Exercises*. One side of the dialectic, the celebrative, focuses on the "working presence of the Lord in a creation seen as made, redeemed, and in process of being transfigured by God"; the other, the pragmatic, "looks more closely into the tangle of human history." He sees the dialectic in the different callings of the teacher and the administrator; the administrator must inevitably "walk the borderline where Church meets the world." As he describes his own experience on that border, we learn what motivated, and what motivates, one of the great Catholic administrators of our age.

The words he cites from Karl Jaspers could summarize his own fifty years as a member of the Society of Jesus:

> It is as though the world wanted itself to be known; as though it were part of our glorification of God in this world to get to know the world with all our God-given faculties, to rethink as it were the thoughts of God, even if we ourselves can never grasp them except as they are reflected in the universe as we know it.[2]

Finding God in the tangle of human history, in one's own experience of that history--that is the pragmatic challenge awaiting one who has felt the power of Ignatius's *Spiritual Exercises*.

In this collection's third essay, William Spohn, S.J. explores Ignatian discernment from the perspective of American pragmatism, "the most distinctive form of American intellectual culture." Father Spohn believes that pragmatists and Jesuit moralists share a "concern for practical effectiveness that is ultimately rooted in a vision of God actively laboring in human experience and history."

Ignatius and American pragmatists would agree, he thinks, that moral discernment is experiential, practical, emotionally charged and transformative. The most important occasions for moral discernment for both are at decision points at life's crossroads. Because emotions play a central role in determining one's course of action at such crossroads, Ignatius's "rules for the discernment of spirits" are especially important, and Father Spohn's exploration of Ignatius's insights only whets the appetite of anyone faced with significant life decisions.

Jeffrey L. Klaiber, S.J. addresses the theme of the series by offering a panoramic view of Latin American history. He suggests that God's labor may be discerned in history, especially in Christians' pursuit of Utopia in opposition to institutions serving an ideology: "Utopia uplifts and dignifies because it is man reaching out to God in his efforts to build the City of God on Earth; but ideology is the closing of the mind to God and to men in the effort to impose a fixed formula on others, usually to the benefit of a few." Father Klaiber makes a convincing case that "the belief that a more just and fraternal society is possible and the hope that it will come to pass have been two fundamental moving forces in the world view of Latin America's popular classes since the sixteenth century." One of the most exciting chapters in this unfolding story is being written even now: "When the bishops of Latin America solemnly committed the church to support the cause of justice and peace by implementing fundamental structural change in society, and later on at Puebla when they called upon Christians to 'opt preferentially for the poor,' they dramatically introduced an entire new chapter in the history of Christianity."

The cost of that commitment is painfully clear in his closing reminder that the day following his speech marked the first anniversary of the savage murder of six Jesuits and two women in El Salvador. Their deaths bring to mind all the Latin American martyrs whose lives and deaths are compelling witnesses to one whose life and death speak to the hearts of all who long for the saving action of God. We are led to realize that the labor of God, like the labor of the mother in childbirth, can be--has been--excruciatingly painful and bloody. Yet that labor is one to which all Christians are called.

In "Church and Culture from a Black Catholic Perspective," Professor Diana Hayes reflects on her own life's journey and her attempts to discern the movement of the Spirit within her. She realizes that, as she began to recognize God's call in her life and to respond haltingly to that call, she was, in effect, "finding her voice," the voice of a black woman, one "whose voice and presence have been marginalized, both because of her race and her sex, in American society and in the Roman Catholic Church." In finding her voice and in making that voice be heard, she experiences a liberation of her self, but also a liberation for others.

That liberation is not without its pain. The voice she raises challenges other women and men who have in different ways oppressed black women to "uncover and vanquish, as best we can, the sins of racism and sexism that persist . . . in our society and in the Church." That challenge requires "excavating the memories of our sojourn in this country," affirming the spirituality and the theology that arise out of this context, and being about the work of God's kingdom.

In this volume's concluding essay, George W. Hunt, S.J. provides a thumbnail sketch of American Catholic journalism as he tells the story of *America* magazine. He sees Jesuit involvement in journalism as perfectly consistent with the mission of the apostles who were called to communicate the good news, the central reality of which is "a mystery of communication: the Word made flesh." Citing Jesuit theologian Avery Dulles, Father Hunt recalls that the Church today "aspires to be a vast international communication network, heeding God's voice in the events of our personal and public history."

As some of the contributors to this volume have sought to heed God's voice in their own stories, or in the stories of oppressed peoples, so *America* magazine seeks in the public arena of contemporary conflict to identify those signs of the times which call for a discernment of spirits and an interpretation in the light of the gospel. As he states it, "we at *America* attempt . . . to inform our readers so that they too might scrutinize, discern, interpret, discover."

Animating the hearts of all Jesuit journalists, Father Hunt believes, is the same meditation that caught the attention of Professor Hayes:

> See all those people on the face of the earth, and such great variety of dress and ways of acting; some are white, some black, some at peace, some at war, some weeping, some laughing, some well, some sick, some coming to birth, some dying. Then listen to what they are saying, how they speak to each other, how they swear and blaspheme. . .

His continuing reflection on the words of Ignatius are a fitting conclusion to these pages of introduction:

> This is the world on which Ignatius is obviously inviting us to reflect, to which Christ will come, and to which we believe he continues to come in 1991. It is a world of endless diversity, a world of moral contrasts, a world worth listening to, and a world worth redeeming.

William J. O'Brien
Assistant to the Dean of Student Affairs

Notes

¹ Peter-Hans Kolvenbach, S.J., *The Characteristics of Jesuit Education* (Washington, D.C.: Jesuit Secondary Education Association, 1987), 17.
² Karl Jaspers, *The Idea of the University*, ed. Karl W. Deutsch (Boston: Beacon Press, 1959), 22.

Leo J. O'Donovan, S.J.

Signs and Choices

Leo J. O'Donovan, S.J. is President of Georgetown University

W e stand at the beginning of another academic year, and in the midst of extraordinary events in the world around us. Only wise men and women can discern which are the most significant signs of such times, read them aright, and guide their choices accordingly. Unhappily, we have grown accustomed to a surfeit of information and symbols in our media age. Science and technology have removed nature from the direct experience of most of us. The "world" of heaven seems more and more like a religious construct of an irretrievable past. What signs are there, in a time of such momentous change, that we can reliably read and then be guided by?

A university, as I see it, is a place of learning and a home for truth. It encourages and enables free inquiry, for the sake of advancing humankind's fragile hold on liberating truth. Above all, I believe, a university should be a community of wisdom. It should be a place where discerning the signs of the times and learning to make wise choices are constant concerns for all its faculty and students, administration and staff.

We are blessed this year at Georgetown to be celebrating two anniversaries that will help us to remember the importance of signs and choices in our lives. With Jesuits and their colleagues throughout the world, we will be celebrating the birth of Ignatius of Loyola in 1491, a full five centuries ago, and the founding of the Society of Jesus in 1540, four hundred fifty years past. For this morning's Mass of the Holy Spirit, I look especially to Ignatius, and for that reason have chosen the texts for his feast day on July 31--the day on which he died, as you may know, and came finally face to face with a God whom all his life he longed to serve more fully.

You all know something of the sixty-five years of Ignatius's life. "The courtier and soldier became the pilgrim and student; the pilgrim and student became priest and apostle; the priest and apostle became the creator of a renowned religious family."[1] We will have ample time this year to become better friends with a man who has had such a momentous impact on the history of the Church and the world.

But it is to Ignatius, the master of discernment and choice, that I suggest we look today. At the turn of the modern age, with one courtly foot still standing in the Middle Ages and the other striding forward into the history of freedom, he is a paradigmatic figure. A man of action and daring, of pragmatic experimentation and constant adaptation, he was also an extraordinary phenomenologist of human consciousness and indeed a mystic as well. Familiar with courts and military campaigns, he longed to walk with the poor Christ and campaign for him. Alert to the power struggles of a new European society, he gave himself entirely to the service of the kingdom of God. A man of action and yet a pioneer of prayer, he was in an exemplary way, as his secretary Polanca said, a contemplative in action.

How did Ignatius see the convulsions of the society, and indeed the desperate need for reform in the Church, around him? In his famous parable of the two standards, but in fact throughout his *Spiritual Exercises*, he saw it as a struggle between the creative power of generous love and the destructive force of selfish pride. Just that simply!

Cutting through the complexity of his expanding world, but without in fact oversimplifying it in any way, he saw how deeply we are all posed with a choice between the two ways which Moses in the Book of Deuteronomy sets before us. There the prophet speaks to the people of Israel for their God:

> See, I have set before you this day life and prosperity, death and disaster... I call heaven and earth to witness against you this day, that I have set before you life and death, blessing and curse.
>
> (Dt 30: 15, 19)

These words were probably used at Israelite liturgies where the people's covenant with Yahweh was made and renewed. They are not at all abstract. They bear on day-to-day relations between members of the people, their call to faithfulness with their God, and the promise of the land which Yahweh has sworn to them.

Beneath and within and beyond all the particular choices that we are daily called to make, Deuteronomy reminds us that we must discern where life is most truly to be found--and choose it, because God is a God of life. Your God, Jesus would later say, is not a God

4

of the dead but of the living, the God of Abraham and Isaac and Jacob.

If Deuteronomy and Ignatius challenge us to discern what is truly good and where real life is to be found, the greater challenge still is to choose and *embrace* the living good. The *Spiritual Exercises* of Ignatius are often interpreted as a school of freedom. In reality, they are far more concerned with liberating our freedom so that we may live for the sake of others and for the glory of the Divine Majesty, as Ignatius was wont to say.

With Peter, as Luke's Gospel describes him, Ignatius saw in Jesus the great sign, the personal presence, the anointed one of God. And not for abstract, other-worldly reasons but because, with Peter, he saw in Jesus the power to save suffering people from the forces of evil. Peter had seen what Jesus did and what he in union with Jesus had been able to do. For Ignatius the choice of the good and of life was fully concretized in his choice to follow Christ, to be a disciple.

The choice was further specified by being, as Luke's Gospel again reminds us, a choice of the cross:

> If anyone wants to be a follower of mine, let him renounce himself and take up his cross every day and follow me. Anyone who wants to save his life will lose it; but anyone who loses his life for my sake, will save it (Luke 9:23-24).

The cross here does not mean the hardships or sufferings of life in general. Rather it means, quite concretely, Jesus' fidelity in word and deed to his proclamation of God's reign in our lives, a reign of justice and love. It means the participation of his disciples in that proclamation. Today it means, surely, the inseparable conjunction of the proclamation of the gospel and the promotion of justice. For Ignatius, the fundamental choice of his life was of someone to follow--not because Ignatius was a passive or insecure person, but because he saw in Jesus of Nazareth, the crucified and risen Lord, someone in whom love gave itself away wholly, consistently, unto the end--and victoriously.

There is still more. Ignatius can teach us to discern what is

5

good in our lives and to choose what is loving, above all because he was convinced at the very center of his being that he himself had been chosen and loved. As Moses urged the people of Israel to walk with their God and choose life, as Jesus calls us after him in his loving way of discipleship, Ignatius reminds us that all good things come to us from God and that we will only truly possess them by offering them back to our Creator in the service of our brothers and sisters. Beyond our discernment and choice is the great liberating fact that we, just as we are, have been accepted and chosen.

Thus we turn not to political analysis or medical research, indispensable as they are. We interrupt our search for the truth and for the good life. We put off the marvelous lectures and other calendar of events scheduled for the year. We stop, chosen and beloved, to worship the God who calls us to life and love. We celebrate the great enduring, unassailable, prevailing sign: the cross of the risen Christ with whom we communicate in every Eucharist. Called by him to the foot of his cross and to the eternal glory of his loving God, in his Spirit we say "Yes" to his way.

His way in our world at its turning point. His example of suffering love. His presence always in our midst. Before which, ultimately, only the silence of adoration is a fitting response.

Note

[1]   William V. Bangert, *A History of the Society of Jesus* (St. Louis: Institute of Jesuit Sources), 45.

Timothy S. Healy, S.J.

Ignatius and the Jesuit Vocation

Timothy S. Healy, S.J. is President of the New York Public Library and former President of Georgetown University.

The topic mercilessly assigned to me on this 450th birthday of the Society of Jesus is one that calls for a scholar or a mystic. After twenty-five years of university administration, I am all too painfully neither. Except for the daily exultation of the Mass, my prayer is on a level with the prayer of Reb Tevye: a long conversation with God, about all the people and places and things of daily life amid a thousand distractions. My only hope is that they do not distract God as much as they do me. And while my scholarship shows that I have learned something since kindergarten, no one could qualify the things I write any more as "serious." So I regard my role this evening as that of introducing more serious offerings; not quite comedy relief, but not all that reassuringly much above it.

I want to start with two quotes and one story, the purpose of which will, I hope, become obvious. The first is a famous passage from *The Aeneid*, Aeneas speaking to Dido as he prepares heartbrokenly to leave Carthage in search of Rome.

> If fate permitted me to spend my days
> By my own lights, and make the best of things
> According to my wishes, first of all
> I should look after Troy and the loved relics
> Left me of my people. Priam's great hall
> Should stand again: I should have restored the tower
> Of Pergamum for Trojans in defeat.[1]

The choice of that text is pretty obvious: Troy and Rome, home and abroad, the known and the threateningly strange, the lost and what is yet to be found, indeed the sacred and the secular.

My second quote comes from John Courtney Murray in a speech he gave at the 125th anniversary of Fordham. "It is the calling of the Jesuit to live on the borderline where the Church meets the world and the world meets the Church."

My story is from the many-volume history of the early Jesuits written by the Spanish historian, Astrain. He tells of a Jesuit provincial in Portugal in the early 1550s who was asked to serve as confessor to the king. The provincial wrote to Ignatius that he intended to turn the job down because it would involve him in the

9

politics, the maneuvering, the social whirl, and the other distractions, some of them dangerous, of the court. That involvement, he said, could well cost him his immortal soul. From the doughty Ignatius he got back a considerable rocket. The founder's message was that one joined the Society of Jesus to serve the Lord God, wherever and however there was hope of that service, and that a preoccupation with the saving of one's soul at the expense of that service was not only unhealthy, but reprehensible.

The point of both quotes and the story is that there is in Jesuit life a deep dialectic that arises essentially from Ignatius's *Spiritual Exercises*. Let me call one side of it "celebration." It focuses, as does the passionately mystical Ignatius, on the working presence of the Lord God in a creation seen as made, redeemed, and in process of being transfigured by God. Modern spokesmen for celebration are Teilhard de Chardin, Henri de Lubac, and Karl Rahner. All of them are rooted in the great final meditation of the *Exercises*, the *Contemplatio ad Amorem*, and recall the spirituality of the Christian East that makes so much of the splendor of God, the glory of God. "All is yours, and you are Christ's, and Christ is God's" is the way St. Paul puts it. When faced with the tough question, "What's the use of that?" Jesuits answer that "Love is not legitimated by its uses, nor is prayer, nor art, nor thought. They are legitimated by the Lord they express."

The other side of Jesuit life can be called "pragmatic," and, while it does not contradict the first, it looks more closely into the tangle of human history, the time and place and people that reveal to us both the presence of God and the will of God. This vision, too, derives from Ignatius, who wanted his sons to turn their hands to anything judged to be useful for "the greater glory of God." The pragmatic is always more complicated and usually controversial. There are Jesuits, like the Portuguese provincial, who tend to the conscience of kings, and others like the Spaniard, Molina, who work out the ground rules for assassinating them. While this Western half of Jesuit spirituality admits that the Lord rises above all creation, it is much struck by the fact that only created reality can reveal that same Lord. When challenged as to what purpose it serves, the Jesuit pragmatist answers, "The half loaf of admittedly half-understood reality may be better than the no bread of sheer idealism, even divine idealism."

In Jesuit tradition we speak of this dichotomy in several ways. We pride ourselves that we are "contemplatives in action." We justify many rather dubious practices by saying that we are "in the world but not of it." A newer slogan describes us as laboring for "faith-justice," which gives this old English teacher the problem that a hyphen is a way to duck explaining a relationship. Very few Jesuits, and most of them geniuses, can bridge these gaps, embody within themselves both great thrusts, lead a life that is one both in inward celebration and outward practicality--save Troy and still find Rome. John Courtney Murray and Father Pedro Arrupe seemed able to turn from one great thrust of Ignatian spirituality to the other without schizophrenia or even embarrassment.

What I say will be understood by all my brethren who have given themselves to the long labor of the professorate or to the restless waters of university administration. Nothing in what I say is meant to disprize the Jesuit vocation as teacher. Our Jewish tradition sees teachers as of crowning importance, not because they are intellectually adept or clever but because their studies, in concert with God, "prevent chaos from coming again, prevent the muting of the creative Word." For that reason, in the Jewish tradition teaching has always been a sacred calling. The gospel tells us that our Lord began "to act and to teach," and in this he really was fulfilling a classic Jewish role and thereby vindicating it. All teaching is profoundly revelatory, it is the celebration of God present to creation, and it leads ultimately to the glory of God. For Jesuit teachers, teaching as the imitation of Christ could hardly have a clearer warrant.

One last personal note, and that concerns not my total of fifty years as a Jesuit, but the actual years that made them up. For those of us for whom the Second Vatican Council came at mid life, its documents sang like the Declaration of Independence must have sounded to middle-aged men and women in Boston and Philadelphia and Charleston in 1776. It was a vast shaking off of age and chains, a renewal of the Church so profound and far-reaching that it took our breath away, a shedding of at least three centuries'

11

encrustation of policy and practice, a "beacon and eternal beam." That was what our minds said and we were right. But I do not think there is any one of us whose heart has not, at one time or another in the hectic days that followed, cried with anguish for one or another practice, place, habit, or way of proceeding. "Mortal trash for the residuary worm," maybe, but it was hard to lose them. The Council was doubly divisive for those of us in higher education because it shed for us so much of our past.

As I look back in the optimism of memory, what strikes me most is the security of those preconciliar years. The Society of Jesus was, like the Church itself, fixed and eternal. The rector sat at his place at table and in chapel, and the order of the day, indeed the order of the years, was spelled out. When I entered in 1940, I knew exactly what I would be doing for the next fifteen years, and I was right. Jesuit life was too interesting and we young were too feisty to be either orderly or serene, but secure it was and we in it. The classics led to philosophy; philosophy in turn was hand-maiden to the queen of the sciences, theology; and theology's culminating moment was the priesthood. There is an old Jesuit joke that in the study of the classics we lost our taste, in the study of philosophy we lost our reason, in the study of theology we lost our faith, and it was the last year that gave them all back again. The losses were not really that bad, but the last year did give us the chance to study the architecture of a great order and to probe at leisure its history and its soul.

Two qualities marked those days. The first was their inwardness; the second, their celebratory and not pragmatic focus. We mirrored the Church itself in the forties and fifties, without realizing that we were in the twilight of the Council of Trent and radically unprepared for what was to come. My picture of that inwardness does not talk down what we did. We ran good colleges. Their enclosed Catholicism was precisely what was needed by generations of the immigrant poor whose access to professions and other leadership roles could be enabled and secured by such training. The real problem was that, as the twentieth century wore on, institutions like Fordham and Georgetown fell further and further behind their secular college peers, in autonomy, in variety, and in research.

After the inward-looking and celebratory nature of Jesuit training, exposure to a good graduate school came as a shock. Here was "the real world" with a vengeance, for all the ambiguity of that silly phrase. It was not that one could not compete, for most of us could. It was just that the daily business of living, the air we breathed, the people we rubbed shoulders with and the faculty we admired pointed us toward a totally different kind of institution. We talked about it, we griped about it, we laughed at it, we loved it, but essentially we brought back to the relatively closed world of Catholic higher education a new set of eyes that were sharper and wider lensed--in fact, relatively the same set of eyes that our lay Catholic colleagues had been bringing to them for years. We also brought back the liveliness and curiosity and energy of the secular university world, joined with its intolerance, its objectivism, and at times its horrible carelessness of the impact of theory and product on human life.

There were two ways that the young Jesuit with his spanking new doctorate could go. The first was the faculty track, essentially the celebration of God in creation, the one I still regard as in the long run the more useful and most likely to work to God's glory. The second was of course the pragmatic one, administration.

Three months after finishing my doctorate I was ensconced as the vice president at Fordham. I told the new president I thought this was a bad idea, despite my seven years of service at the university. His answer was not particularly complimentary, but it was decisive, since he was also the rector. He said, "You may be right, but you're all I've got." With that I began to walk the borderline where the Church meets the world.

I was not on the job six months when a new public law put the cat among the pigeons. The State of New York proposed to give direct and unrestricted institutional aid to its colleges and universities based on the number of degrees they awarded. The amounts were serious, and it was perfectly clear that, if Fordham could not qualify for that aid, it could not survive on any intellectual level it would regard as respectable and probably would have had difficulty surviving at all. On the other hand, the State of New York had as part of its Constitution the infamous Blaine Amendment, prohibiting any direct or indirect aid to any religious institution--far more restrictive than the federal Constitution. It must have pleased Blaine's undistinguished shade that, almost a century after his death, his legal artifact was still plaguing Roman Catholics. Fordham retained Walter Gelhorn, a distinguished Columbia professor, to study the matter, and he came up with a report to the university after six delightful months during which he was on campus three or four times a week. He told Fordham to change the state registration under which it was tax exempt and to re-register, not as a religious institution but as a university. He told it to take seriously its theology, seriously enough to require theology of all students, not just of Catholics; to keep all religious observances, but not make them mandatory except on ceremonial occasions; to assure that the university had an autonomous board of directors, whatever its internal composition. In other words, the recommendation of the report made high secular good sense, and also urged the university in just those ecumenical directions that the Vatican Council had made the official teaching of the Church.

You can imagine the uproar within Catholic circles. The magazine *America* roundly condemned the leadership of the university and cast the report into outer darkness. If it had had teeth, it would have gnashed them. The charge was, of course, that the president was "secularizing" Fordham. Some of it was really comic. It made absolutely no difference to the state whether Fordham achieved its tax exemption as a Church or as a university; Professor Gelhorn merely suggested that it ought to make some difference to Fordham. At the time, the university had one of the best theological faculties in the Church, men and women eminently able to make their subject stand as an autonomous intellectual discipline and not as a tool of indoctrination for baptized Catholics. The legal separation of the Jesuit community from the university came from another source, but was included in the general resentment and became the object of cries of outraged virtue on both Right and Left. Pulpits thundered, archbishops growled, Jesuits fulminated, but the institutional imperative for survival predictably won out. Fordham and almost every Catholic college in the state qualified for state aid. Despite the warnings and dire forebodings, only one of the eighty Catholic institutions secularized itself and ceased to be Catholic. That process, which took about a year and a half, was my baptism--the first fruits of a vocation suddenly gone pragmatic.

In five or six places in northern Europe and North America, the Church finds herself in cohabitation with universities that enjoy the full secular reality of their being. Whatever else they are, they are clearly acknowledged by their peers as universities with all the rights and responsibilities that come with the title. In each of these institutions, the Church has indeed a privileged position; it is welcomed, allowed the full range of its pastoral services and liturgy, and has access to the life and learning of the university. Each of these universities by its very nature lives that edgy border between Church and world; and, because they are universities, they are subject to all the disputes, the tensions, the troublesome tugging and pulling that mark the life of the Church whenever she ties herself clearly to time and place. Georgetown is emphatically one of these institutions.

The first strenuous service these universities do for the Church is to introduce her to the young, particularly to the talented young. Bright-eyed and bushy-tailed, they descend each fall and they bring a host of good things--energy, curiosity, and, of course, beauty. But they also bring a massive inexperience that in one sense is the delight of the faculty, but, in another, its despair. We like to say, "Let's not reinvent the wheel," but that frozen bit of wisdom does not apply to an undergraduate college. For the young, the problem of controlled motion around a fixed point has to be presented, argued, and discovered all over again pretty much every year. There are only so many times when the normally equipped human being can argue out the problem of evil without resorting to Luther's exasperated comment, "Tell them Dr. Martin Luther will have it so." These arguments regularly find their way into the student press and at times into the larger press in plain public view. The university's reminder to the Church is that this particular border is one of constant discovery of what has already been discovered, of unending argument about positions the Church quite rightly regards as essentially settled.

Such argument leads us to another problem. If argument is

rational, it means that one side does not always win or, at least, that it does not win yet. Young Catholics are capable of rejecting Church teaching as well as accepting it. Time and experience may well change that rejection, and in many cases do. But as long as the Church lives cheek by jowl with a university, it must accept two of the university's great presuppositions. The first is that all assumptions are open to question, all formulations challengeable. The second is that the instruments with which the question or challenge is worked out are reason and argument. A university keeps its anathemas only for those who thwart this process, for instance, by cheating. Resistance to Church teaching will at times take obvious and organized form. The Catholic press howls about the presence of "pro-choice" marchers from Catholic campuses because it does not understand that within a university the only way to present the Church's position is as one of many choices and then to argue for its acceptance. The struggle is not neat, it is not tidy, and it is not and cannot be always successful.

Another interesting spot on the border is academic freedom and academic freedom is most likely to be challenged when a Church is present. We are now on faculty terrain, but the questioning of assumptions is not a university stance reserved only to students. An essential part of any university's being is the freedom of its faculty to explore, to investigate, to publish, and to teach. This freedom remains as a great good, obviously not an absolute, but still a major aspect of the university's being. The occasional shock and scandal it can cause are, in the university's view, and in the view of most of our fellow citizens, minor inconveniences that flow from a major good. The Church, however, while it has no difficulty arguing for the greater good, frequently finds it hard to impossible to settle for the lesser evil. It is all too easy in that mindset to focus an attack on one individual, on a particular annoyance or a set of them, and in one's zeal to forget that you can hardly reform a temple by pulling it down. All too often the first victim of religious intellectual intransigence is charity.

Theology in university terms is always a process, not a product. Another kind of hurt occurs, both ways, when the Church presents propositions and conclusions that have not been adequately worked

16

out by the learned disciplines they either derive from or affect. A perfect example is the moral reasoning, absolutely unexceptionable and in fact extremely beautiful, with which the Church approaches the debate about the sanctity of life. Such propositions and conclusions, however, depend in their application, at least in large part, upon the findings of science and the Church frequently does not allow scientists to influence the definitions. One thinks of the long conflict between modern biblical scholarship and what used to be called the Roman Biblical Commission. Text by text, the scholars disassembled and reassembled the Church's understanding of the great deposit of the Word of God. The Church stood to her guns manfully throughout the whole process and so did the biblicists. But under that double pressure the ground of scriptural study shifted sharply, and the resulting depth and beauty that we now enjoy we owe to a great deal of hard work accompanied by many hard words. The wrestle over biblical scholarship, at times in fact an open warfare, benefited both the scholars and the Church and makes a paradigm we ought not to forget. Form criticism may seem many country miles distant from *in vitro* fertilization, but the intellectual dynamics of the border are much the same in either case, despite the fact that subject, vocabulary, and the embattled warriors have all changed.

There is another problem on that border that I, as an American, think important. Years ago, when he founded Georgetown, John Carroll wrote to Rome that "the good effects of freedom of religion are beginning to be felt." In that sentence he captured an essential element of our life as a people and one under which the Church herself has thrived. American Catholics feel that not enough of this experience is either understood or accepted within the universal Church.

One major piece of that experience is our understanding of law. Heirs to the tiny island that the Church gave away in the Reformation, clearly in the interests of the Holy Roman Empire, Americans look on all law, civil and ecclesiastical, as a floor, not as a ceiling. Law sets up minimal requirements, and most Americans feel by and large that morality begins when law stops. To those brought up under either Roman law or its Napoleonic derivative, the law is as much a teacher as it is a police officer. It is the function of Roman law to serve as ceiling; to hold up ideals of conduct and being; to instruct, invite, and inspire. Americans who see the law as meant to define, to command, and to set minimum standards thus find themselves in sharp conflict with that European vision. Americans are generally puzzled because they feel they have on their side not only Aquinas's teaching but also John Henry Newman's reading of the Church's dogmatic development through her many centuries, while Europeans are frustrated because their concept of law more resembles the Book of Numbers, revealed from on high, immutable and all inclusive. This dispute in all its various forms is at least the equal of the long wrestle over scriptural interpretation and will probably take as long to resolve as did the endless quarrel about usury as a moral evil.

Let me now turn to another dimension of Jesuit pragmatism, one that involves fewer of us but that has over the centuries been a significant part of Jesuit service to the Church. I am speaking of those who for any length of time have lived and worked outside of ecclesiastical works and in secular ones. Father Robert Drinan's ten years in the American Congress allowed him, under another rubric, to bring a Catholic understanding to bear on Latin American relations, on immigration, on criminal justice, and on the treatment of the poor--areas that few Jesuits are able to touch except through research and writing. Bob put his life and his career where his prayer led him. How significant and how important that service was has yet to be chronicled. His pragmatic Jesuit spirituality enabled him, in response to a disciplinary decision of the Church, simply and without fuss to resign. We Jesuits seldom speak in public of how proud we can be of one another. My pride in Bob's Ignatian service and equally Ignatian resignation goes beyond any skill I have in words.

The seven years before I came to Georgetown, I was the academic vice-chancellor of the City University of New York. The job was the consequence of trying to set up a liberal arts college in Bedford-Stuyvesant. It was impossible to get the money for it and I ultimately reported to the Provincial and his advisors that, if Jesuits were to be significantly involved in the education of the poor, some of them had to be committed to the public sector. I was at the time battling an official at York College who kept telling me that I was "overqualified," a concept I have never even been dimly able to understand, when the chancellor offered me the job. I ducked answering until I had a chance to talk to the provincial, who was at that moment on vacation. So I went out to Long Island, and the provincial (who was then Father Robert Mitchell), Father Donald Monan (now president of Boston College), and I walked up and down the beach in our bathing suits and carried on a very typical Jesuit conversation. Don argued that I should take the position, I argued that I should not (as being too showy, too prominent, and perhaps ineffective). The provincial heard us out and finally said "Why not try it?" The Society's purpose was perfectly clear to all three of us. It wanted some of its members involved in the education of the poor, as witnesses to the Church's care, concern, and willingness to help.

The experience was one of the most interesting and enjoyable I have ever had. CUNY is a marvelous place, tough, unpretentious to the point of being at times uncouth, low in style, but long on thought and great care. I learned from it how to serve the dispossessed, and during those seven years that I was of some help at both making and delivering that service. Probably the way it showed most was that when I came to Georgetown I brought with me a real urgency about minority enrollments (not then a settled attitude in most Jesuit institutions). I had learned it from CUNY and from its good men and women who taught me more about my trade than I thought I could learn.

My other secular job, the one I now hold, puts me with a great institution every bit as important as CUNY and almost as complicated. When it became obvious that the New York Public Library wanted me as its president, I talked to the provincial and we had another typically Jesuit conversation. I had worked out carefully on paper all the pros and all the cons, discussed them with several Jesuits here at Georgetown and elsewhere, and went through them for the provincial. When I had finished, he said to me, "What do you want?" I made him laugh by telling him that after forty-nine years I thought I had a right to be told. He agreed and said, "I'll call you in a couple of days." Then he called and said, "If you are offered the job, go ahead and take it."

Once again, the Society's purpose was clear. A principle element was service to the poor through eighty-two branches, many of them located in the poorest parts of the city and all of them, in some two hundred languages, serving the entire body of citizens but, most particularly, those whose access to reading is through libraries, not bookstores. It is a major social distinction. As always, nothing Jesuit is simple and the Order also wanted me to bear witness to the Church's concern and care for high scholarship and to its willingness to defend the freedom, autonomy, and value of human learning. Faith is therefore served by honoring God's creatures, and justice by serving the poor.

I have taken this detour through biography because, to my nonabstractive mind, the only way one can explain anything like the pragmatic half of a Jesuit vocation is historically. I spoke before of Reb Tevye and in his honor quoted the haunting words of Virgil about Troy and Rome. All the years have left me with a wonder and a suspicion. I wonder whether my brethren who have lived their lives in celebration of the Lord God ever yearn to look with the eyes of John Ormond's stone mason, to stand before some work, admittedly of time but of permanence like stone, and mutter, "I bloody did that." Deep in my heart I do not think they do, just as deep in his heart Reb Tevye knew he would never be a wealthy man. I suspect they know as well as I do that we pragmatists will always stand in need of God's much mercy. We may or may not found Rome, but we have lost Troy. On our side of the dichotomy within the Jesuit vocation we can share only in mind and imagination, never in memory, the vision of Karl Jaspers:

> If I ask myself where all this knowledge is headed for, I can only answer in metaphorical terms. It is as though the world wanted itself to be known; as though it were part of our glorification of God in this world to get to know the world with all our God-given faculties, to rethink as it were the thoughts of God, even if we ourselves can never grasp them except as they are reflected in the universe as we know it.[2]

Let me finish with a story that has always enchanted me. A Jesuit provincial once was involved in an automobile accident. He recovered slowly. During his recuperation a Jesuit friend visited him and asked, "Well, Joe, were you ready to meet God?" The provincial thought a moment and answered, "It wasn't God I was worried about. It was Ignatius."

Notes

¹ Virgil, *The Aeneid*, trans. Robert Fitzgerald (New York: Random House, 1983), 107-108.

² Karl Jaspers, *The Idea of the University*, ed. Karl W. Deutsch (Boston: Beacon Press, 1959), 22.

Quotations that are unidentified in this text, some of its terminology, and many of its ideas are all borrowed from an unpublished essay by Peter Steele, S.J.: "Pillar of Smoke, Pillar of Fire: Notes on the Life of the Mind in the Society." Father Steele bears no responsibility for my use of them.

William C. Spohn, S.J.

Pragmatism and the Glory of God: An American Reading of Ignatian Discernment

William C. Spohn, S.J. is Associate Professor of Theological Ethics at the Jesuit School of Theology at Berkeley.

In this five hundredth anniversary of the birth of St. Ignatius of Loyola and the four hundred fiftieth anniversary of the founding of the Society of Jesus, Jesuit institutions are reflecting on their heritage. In his lecture in this series on "The Labor of God: An Ignatian View of Church and Culture," Father Timothy Healy mentioned that pragmatism and the glory of God come together in the Jesuit calling to be "contemplatives in action." He eloquently recounted his history in administration as an example of the pragmatic side of the Jesuit charism. I want to take a different tack by focusing attention on an important part of that Jesuit heritage: moral "discernment," that is, the use of memory, imagination, emotion, and intellect to discover the appropriate action. We will look at Ignatian discernment through the perspective of pragmatism, the most distinctive form of American intellectual culture.

Have you ever noticed how stories about Jesuits cast them in pragmatic terms? There is the one about the Dominican, Franciscan, and Jesuit playing golf on their day off. The foursome ahead of them takes forty-five minutes to play the first hole and another fifty minutes to get to the third green. The good fathers are now irate and go to the clubhouse to talk to the local professional. To their complaints, the pro says, "Relax, fathers, you have to realize those people are blind. They've learned to play golf with total independence. They have to grope for the ball, so it takes them some time."

The Dominican replies, "Isn't it wonderful how God is glorified in his creatures, using their reason to overcome such obstacles!"

The Franciscan says, "Oh, those poor people! My heart just goes out to them. Think of the lives they've lived. How they must have suffered and borne the cross of Christ!"

The Jesuit says, "Couldn't they play at night?"

Jesuits may not want to be associated with pragmatists: what, after all, does the somewhat disreputable term "pragmatism" have to do with the lofty Ignatian purpose of serving "the greater glory of God"? First, some historical clues. The Society of Jesus has achieved more widespread success in university and secondary education in the United States than in any other modern culture. Could there be some affinity between the practical, enterprising

25

spirit of American culture and Jesuit spirituality that accounts in part for this success?

Second, both pragmatists and Jesuits have regularly been accused of holding that "the end justifies the means." As one old Jesuit professor put it, "If the end doesn't justify the means, I don't know what does!" And William James scandalized the philosophical fraternity by insisting that truth was no more than the "cash value" of ideas. That catchy phrase stuck in the popular mind and gave pragmatism a rather seedy reputation as the philosophy of crass opportunism, a reputation that flourishes mostly among those who have never read a word of the pragmatists.

Blaise Pascal took seventeenth century Jesuit casuists to task for abandoning divine moral principles in their flexibility at finding solutions for their worried penitents.[1] The Vatican is expected to publish a document on moral theology that will condemn "proportionalism," the twentieth century offspring of casuistry, for tolerating evil for the sake of good ends with that same jesuitical flexibility. And who are the ringleaders of the proportionalists? Richard McCormick, Josef Fuchs, and Bruno Schüller, all of the Society of Jesus. Like William James and John Dewey, they do not hold for absolute moral norms or intrinsically evil acts but insist that morality means balancing the values and disvalues of the actual situation in order to produce the best results.

What accounts for this unholy alliance between pragmatists and Jesuit moralists? I believe that it can be traced to their common concern for practical effectiveness that is ultimately rooted in a vision of God actively laboring in human experience and history.[2] American pragmatists mine the same region of human experience that Ignatius Loyola did. They provide a philosophical rationale for the intuitions of this practical religious genius. Ignatius has a few suggestions to make to American pragmatists, as well, not only to James and Dewey but to all of us insofar as we share their preference for an approach to meaning that is experiential, practical, emotionally charged, and transformative. Before we consider each of these in turn, let us look briefly at the ex-soldier turned pilgrim, Ignatius of Loyola.

Ignatius was a man of action rather than of speculation.

Despite what is commonly supposed, he did not found the Society of Jesus to refute Martin Luther's Reformation but to preach the gospel and renew Christian life. He was not a systematic thinker but a director of souls and, eventually, the organizer of a community that broke the mold of religious life by preferring to find God in the marketplace rather than in the monastery. The community's basic purpose was "the ministry of the Word" and direct works of mercy that validated it, a message to repent and change one's life for Christ. His two written works, *The Spiritual Exercises* and *The Constitutions of the Society of Jesus*, are resolutely practical--not arguments about truth but handbooks for action. They aim to help individuals and communities discover where God is calling them in concrete circumstances that often call for adjusting plans. Finally, the education of the early Jesuits concentrated on rhetoric and communication more than on science or speculation. It makes sense that the best known and most typical Jesuits have been activists like Francis Xavier and the subversive Elizabethan Edmund Campion rather than the great mathematician Clavius. Even when Ignatius's sons have been speculative giants, their concerns have usually been practical: Karl Rahner claiming that the grace of God could be experienced or John Courtney Murray trying to show that Roman Catholics could embrace American freedom of religion and conscience.

Let us now look at practical moral reflection through the eyes of Ignatius and various American pragmatists. We will take up in turn the common denominators of moral discernment: it is experiential, practical, emotionally charged, and transformative.

Discernment is experiential.

Discernment is experiential: insightful, sensual, and active. Moral philosophers are probably frustrated reading Ignatius and the pragmatists. They do not begin their discussion of morality with principles and rules; indeed, they seldom refer to general moral principles at all. Values arise in *experience*, which is the vital interaction between our interests and the stubborn resistance of everyday reality. They presume that moral rules set the outer limits of action, but rules do not dictate how to act in response to the

27

unique contours of the present problem. Knowing that there are guiderails on the side of the road will not teach us how to drive. Driving is a skill that requires clear senses, adaptable reflexes, and practical memory--and so does moral discernment. Moral discernment grows by trial and error in sorting out experience that is often a buzzing, blooming mass of confusion, as James put it.

Meaning, which is the truth that we need to live, does not emerge automatically from ordinary experience. Ignatius began his schooling in discernment while convalescing from a leg shattered at the siege of Pamplona. With nothing better to do, he whiled away the hours reading the Andrew Greeley novels of his day. He noticed that reading stories about the mighty deeds of knights in armor left him feeling flat, restless, bored, but reading the lives of the saints fired his heart with a different sort of emotion. Led by great dreams and bold impulses in the early months after his conversion, he made enough mistakes to last a lifetime. Delusory visions and false consolation led to austerities and severe fasts that left his digestion damaged for life. Looking back later, he determined that his followers should not be swept up in austere penances and fasting-- a portion of his legacy to which Jesuits have been quite faithful.

He began to notice when he had been tricked and when he had been led by "the Spirit of God." From those experiences eventually came his *Spiritual Exercises*. They are a program of religious experiments that are geared to teach others similar skill in sorting out meaning from illusion and temptation in ideas, feelings, and religious experiences.

Jonathan Edwards, a Puritan pastor, is the genius who stands at the source of American theology and philosophy, including pragmatism. In his classic work, *Religious Affections* (1745), Edwards describes twelve signs of genuine religious experience to those who had been touched by the intense period of the Great Awakening that swept the colonies from 1740-43.[3] Had their conversions been genuine or false? Why had so many promising beginnings come to nothing only a few years later? Since in Puritan theology only those who had been authentically converted were saved, this was a question of eternal life or death.

Even though Edwards considered Jesuits to be among the

lowest forms of papist idolaters, his account of religious experience echoes many of the insights found in Ignatius. Both agree that when people are truly converted to God, their experience changes. Edwards held that God grants to the convert a new sensibility, a new capacity for perception that is analogous to sight or taste. The convert perceives an entirely new phenomenon, the beauty of God in nature, doctrines, and actions. The unconverted can only appreciate God in an impersonal way, as great and powerful but not as good and caring. This new relish conveys the full meaning of the truths of faith; it provides "sensible" and not merely "notional" knowledge, "as he that has perceived the sweet taste of honey, knows much more about it, than he who has only looked upon and felt it."[4] Sensual meaning captures more of reality than concepts can.

As the person matures in the Spirit, this new taste for God's beauty actively helps in discerning what to do. The convert takes delight in genuinely good actions and inclines to do them. However, "if an unworthy unholy action be suggested to it, its sanctified taste relishes no sweetness in it, but on the contrary is nauseous to it."[5]

In the *Exercises*, Ignatius encourages the person making the retreat to seek a similar sensual knowledge. The person should seek "spiritual relish and fruit" in the meditations, "for it is not knowing much, but realizing and relishing things interiorly, that contents and satisfies the soul."[6] The deepest sort of human meaning is neither heat without light nor light without heat, but is insightful and richly affective at the same time.[7]

Discernment is practical.

Discernment is practical because the most important choices we make are not theoretical. Ignatius and the pragmatists focus on the same decisions: particular choices that determine the sort of person we will become. In these "life choices" the option is not between good and evil or between following a commonly accepted moral rule or breaking it. The *Spiritual Exercises* are a series of meditations and conversation for people at a crossroads who need to decide what path to follow. They want to know whether one of their options contains the gracious invitation of God. That question is too practical for most systems of ethics. At most such systems can offer universal rules which should guide anyone faced with a similar choice. But in discerning a life choice, the question is not about anyone, but about this particular person in these particular circumstances. Ethics can tell me what is right and good, but ethics cannot dictate what is *appropriate* for this unique moment. Discernment seeks a more specific insight.

According to James, the fundamental moral situation is one in which the specific judgments we have to make are "in unprecedented cases and lonely emergencies," where common moral maxims do not apply, "and the hidden oracle alone can speak. . ."[8] We must decide not only what to do but who to become. The most basic practical challenge, therefore, is to give the self a definite shape:

> The issue here is one of utmost pregnancy, for it decides a man's entire career. When he debates, Shall I commit this crime? choose that profession? accept that office, or marry this fortune?--his choice really lies between one of several equally possible future Characters. What he shall *become* is fixed by the conduct of this moment.[9]

How then do we hear what "the hidden oracle" is saying? We determine whether our options are realistic. We consult our past experience and future expectations, our memories, hopes and fears to shed some light on this unique moment of choice. The abstractions of ethics are too general for the complex setting of action. We have to evaluate it concretely through factual data, practical reason, emotion, and analogy. The situation of a life choice is unique because it is unrepeatable: the person who makes the decision will never stand at this crossroads again. If I decide not to marry my fiancé or not to become a physician, I will be a different person because I will have opted for a different character, a different future.

The appropriate choice is not necessarily the one that is the most ideal or the most heroic. Ignatius pointed out that good persons are tempted by the appearance of good rather than by grossly immoral options. The most ideal choice may be attractive because of unacknowledged guilt or a hidden desire for praise. Following that road would lead the individual to move beyond grace and might end in disillusion and disaster.

Ignatius sees three ways of discerning a life choice: by direct, undeniable religious experience, by weighing the deep emotions that the options engender in us, and by rationally considering which option is a better means to the goal of serving God and saving our souls. Even though for centuries Jesuits favored the rational approach, Ignatius himself preferred the method of discerning through affectivity. He recommended the rational approach only when affectivity was flat; and even then the decision made by balancing the pros and cons had to be confirmed by the peace, joy, and consolation that come from God.[10] He is not denigrating rationality in favor of emotion because, in discernment about practical matters, rationality needs the felt assessment that only mature emotion can give.

This approach echoes John Dewey's account of practical deliberation. Because Dewey held that truth is instrumental, some have thought that he was only interested in calculating the most expeditious means to the end. In fact, for him deliberation relies more on the felt appreciation of the qualities inherent in the options than on instrumental rationality. It is "a dramatic rehearsal (in imagination)." We let each option project its future career on the screen of imagination to feel its "quality," its felt sense of value. Then we compare it with the felt sense of value in the other options. "In thought as well as in overt action, the objects experienced in following out a course of action attract, repel, satisfy, annoy, promote and retard."[11]

How can we judge whether these commitments will be right and true? James insisted that the only proof is living them out. Experience must confirm or refute the fundamental commitments we make in life: does God exist? is life worth living? is the universe indifferent to morality? We cannot resolve these issues theoretically; and failure to make a choice about them is itself a choice. If I decide to live as if God does not exist, I may well close myself off to the very experiences that would challenge my agnosticism.

Pragmatism's basic thesis is that all truth is practical, instrumental, and provisional.[12] Ignatius did not worry about such things, but he certainly held that practical decisions call for honest and searching discernment. We have to get the facts right so that our options are realistic; no religious experience can substitute for that. Once that task is accomplished, however, emotions become central in determining what specific course of action we are called to do, what option is the will of God, not in general, but for us here and now.

James and Ignatius are expressing what mature people already do when making decisions. I remember going to a Trappist monastery in California twenty years ago with some other young Jesuits to give the monks a workshop in Ignatian discernment. (It said a great deal about their humility that they listened to us--also a good deal about ours, since we were not aware of the irony!) We said that Ignatius was only formalizing a process that Christians already followed in their lives.

We asked the monks to reflect on a recent decision they had made and see whether it had unconsciously followed the Ignatian rules for discernment. When the time came to recount these experiences to the group, one of the monks said, "You are probably right about discernment, but to tell the truth, I can't remember when the last time was that I made a decision. When you get to my age, ideas that are from the Lord are just easy to welcome and those that aren't from God just drop off; you just let them go without much fuss."

I blushed interiorly and thought, "I'm giving a workshop on discernment to this man?" I found out later that he had been Thomas Merton's spiritual director for several years. This monk had such well-tuned "religious affections" that he spontaneously did what the rest of us have to do reflectively and methodically. His wisdom, his graceful "walking in the Spirit," came from a lifetime of intimacy and fidelity. Those of us who are beginners have to be a lot more programmatic about discernment.

Discernment focuses on emotions

Discernment focuses on emotions because they are the origins of action and its key guide . Ignatius and all the pragmatists would agree with Jonathan Edwards's conviction that "affections [are] the springs that set men going in all the affairs of life, and engage them in all their pursuits."[13] Most of them would also agree that unless the affections are converted, they lead to disaster. Because there is

32

no divorce between rationality and affectivity, our emotions have to be grounded in the truth to be trustworthy. Our deep emotions have a logic and orientation that direct our action; however, they must be transformed by exposure to ultimate value or they can be blind guides.

The Great Awakening set the pattern for American religious life that still lingers in the domesticated versions of "born again" Christianity. Living an upright moral life will not bring anyone to human fulfillment; that requires conversion to God whose grace is manifest in Jesus Christ. An authentic religious conversion does not happen serenely; usually it comes with an emotional struggle and breakthrough that catapults the convert into a new life. Unfortunately, American Christianity has often ignored the quieter sorts of conversions which are more like the coming of spring than the sun bursting through thick clouds.

To the critics who condemned the Awakening for being emotionally overwrought, Edwards had one reply: "True religion, in great part, consists in holy affections."[14] He conceded the dangers: many were fooled because they thought that the more intense or sudden or elated the emotion was the more surely it came from God. But the greater danger lay with the cold-hearted rationalists who had all the answers and none of the heart for this religion of love. If they had actually experienced the compelling beauty of God, how could they remain aloof and indifferent? Most likely because they were unconverted, still "carnal," unspiritual beings incapable of rising above self-interest. Only the lure of God's beauty could crack open the self-centered heart and empower it to see the goodness and the needs of others.[15] Morality gets transformed by this reorientation. The lure of beauty pulls the person into action; duty is no longer the push from behind.

When God's personal goodness and beauty are disclosed to people, their value systems are reoriented. If they are faithful in responding to the gospel in the midst of inevitable trials, they will gradually develop a taste for goodness and will experience delight in doing good as a gravitational pull. Human values will become transparent to the divine beauty hidden in them: here Edwards shows a sacramental sense that is unusual for a Puritan, but it

33

certainly converges with Ignatius's hope of "finding God in all things."[16] God is not found by deserting the suffering world and ascending some mountaintop. The journey leads in the opposite direction: we find God in the needs of others, in the struggle to bring a new world to birth.

Ignatius would agree with Edwards that a person's affections and dispositions play the central role in conversion and in discernment.[17] He writes that "spiritual exercises" mean "every way of preparing and disposing the soul to rid itself of all disordered tendencies, and, after it is rid, to seek and find the Divine Will as to the management of one's life for the salvation of the soul. . . "[18] If the retreat director finds early in the month-long period of prayer that the retreatant is dominated by basic tendencies that are not ordered to God, the director must end the retreat. The person is encouraged to a reformation of life and sent home because that person lacks the capacity for learning discernment. The heart must be firmly set on "the glory of God," that is, the praise, reverence, and service of God that comes in the healing of men and women and their world. Without being set on the Kingdom of God, the heart has no moral compass. Lacking this goal to function as its "magnetic north," it cannot pragmatically discover the means that lead to the goal. The lofty purpose becomes the most practical touchstone for moral decision because it sets the heart in the right direction.

Ignatius gives one set of "Rules for the Discernment of Spirits" for directing the unconverted and another for directing those who are committed to God, because their basic affective patterns are different. Most of us have heard people say, "I am comfortable with this... I feel good about this" concerning actions that we find very troubling. We should not tell people who are unconverted to follow their feelings because their feelings are the problem! Their affective tendencies are misdirected to false values such as pleasure, greed, and pride. In contrast, those who have experienced God's radical peace and consolation and are committed to seek greater closeness to God have the affective touchstone to discern God's call in their ideas, feelings, and religious experiences.[19] They will sense the goal they long for in the paths that lead to it.

Our values are encoded in our affective software, our moral character, and they operate through our habits. Discernment uses the sense of who we are and what we stand for as the touchstone to determine the value of the various options we face. Ignatius and the pragmatists tells us that the agreement between character and appropriate action registers as a felt *harmony*. Options that express our deepest hopes and values will be harmonious with them; those that do not will be out of tune. Some of us may grow to be as wise as that old Trappist monk whose heart was so perfectly tuned to God's Spirit. On the other hand, people who are obsessed with pleasure, hungry for power, or defensively fearful cannot appreciate the call of Christ to compassion, service, and trust. Because that call does not harmonize with their basic values, it must seem naive, threatening, or silly.

But what about those more favorably disposed to the call of Christ? Are they supposed to be attracted to the hardships of poverty or to being dismissed by others as religious fanatics? For Ignatius, there is no value in these trials unless they are experienced in connection with Christ. He labors in the world to overcome oppression and violence, to set the captives free. We become his companions by working alongside him, sharing his sufferings and triumphs. The cost of discipleship becomes less frightening when we find intimacy with Christ in the struggle. Those who stand on the sidelines not only miss the fight; they miss the Lord as well.[20]

The whole pedagogy of the *Exercises* as "the school of the affections" centers on this reversal of values. Ignatius expects the retreatant to feel the tug of war between the lure of riches, honors, and pride, and the gospel values of poverty, humiliation, and service. The retreatant should learn the skill of discernment from this conflict, this "movement of spirits," just as Ignatius did early in his conversion. This pedagogy of the affections involves recognizing favorite patterns of self-deception and compromise, balancing times of elation and times of discouragement, and learning to relish the goodness of living with Christ.

The affections get educated, change, in large part when the imagination is retooled. Many days of the retreat are spent reflecting on the scenes of Christ's life to deepen the hold of his values on the heart. As the retreatant comes to enter into the story of Jesus and make it his or her own story, the stories set a pattern for a new identity. Gospel scenes become scenarios for action, paradigms that guide the affections to appropriate responses and choices. Compassion, for instance, gets a specific scenario for action from contemplating the Good Samaritan; no one who has assimilated that parable can look at the homeless with indifference. Gradually, a matrix of Christian values becomes central in the person's heart; that matrix will serve as the affective norm to guide the fundamental decision that the retreatant will make.

Unlike Dewey or James, who did not stand within the Christian tradition, other classic American thinkers do appeal to the story of Christ as the basic pattern for the affections. Edwards expected that genuine religious affections would promote the characteristic values of Christ's temperament ("love, meekness, quietness, forgiveness and mercy") because the Spirit of Christ dwelt in the hearts of Christians.[21] Josiah Royce in his later, more pragmatic writings found the basic moral principle in loyalty to the cause of Christ, that is, reconciliation of all persons in the universal "Beloved Community."[22] H. Richard Niebuhr's ethics of responsibility employs the story of Jesus Christ as the primary symbol that guides Christian response to God.[23]

Dewey and James do not see the necessity of a profound reorientation of values. Although they make human interests, desires, and purposes the starting points of action, they do not always see them as egocentric. In addition, they seem not to appreciate the role of language and community symbols in shaping the affections.[24] On the side of the agent, they rely on a sense of harmony between our deepest felt values and our explicit intentions to judge the moral quality of action.[25] On the side of action, success is the more significant test of interests and ideas. Do these interests and desires need to be converted religiously? Certainly not for John Dewey.

However, James might reply that transformation is needed, even though outside *The Varieties of Religious Experience* he did not show much interest in religious conversion. As a young man he experienced a psychological conversion that led him out of a long period of depression and paralysis.[26] In the *Varieties*, he finds two affective stances to be inadequate: morality as a grim devotion to duty that eventually grows weary, and "healthy-minded" optimism that ignores the evil in the world. He favors the realism of the "twice-born" who have struggled through despair and find the grounds for hope and moral renewal in a chastened faith.[27]

Discernment is transformative.

Discernment is transformative because its final test is effectiveness in changing a frustrating situation. Pragmatism's boldest claim is that all truth is practical: ideals become true only when they make experience more satisfactory. James writes that a new idea "makes itself true, gets itself classed as true, by the way it works..."[28] We start thinking because something in our environment is not working, something is blocking our vital needs and interests. If we lived in a universe alone and without any frustration, we would never begin to think.[29] We keep reflecting and acting until that blockage is resolved; further action faces new challenges and the process begins again.

William James saw the world of experience as full of challenge, a universe "half-wild and half-saved."[30] Its course is not all worked out in the mind of God, as the idealists imagined. The world becomes what we make of it. We add to the sum of emerging meaning by our efforts or subtract from it by our fears and cowardice. Courage and faith have a common root in the readiness to act when we do not know the outcome. James believed that we have to live strenuously and energetically, even if that energy brings pain.

In the end, our contributions to the struggle have cosmic significance; they change both the world we live in and God. James had known depression and the temptation of suicide; nevertheless, he asserted that life was worth living:

> God himself, in short, may draw vital strength and increase of very being from our fidelity. For my part, I do not know what the sweat and blood and tragedy of this life mean, if they mean anything

short of this. If this life be not a real fight, in which something is eternally gained for the universe by success, it is no better than a game of private theatrics from which one may withdraw at will. But it feels like a real fight,--as if there were something really wild in the universe which we, with all our idealities and faithfulnesses, are needed to redeem; and first of all to redeem our own hearts from atheisms and fears.[31]

Jesuit pragmatism agrees that life is a struggle that requires our best efforts. Jesuit pragmatism may be more hopeful about the outcome than is James, but it appreciates the "real fight" we are in here and now. Both Ignatius and James were fond of military metaphors to express life's challenges. Jesuit pragmatism recognizes that the glory of God breaks into the world with difficulty because it knows the story of the cross and resurrection. "The light shines forth in the darkness, and the darkness cannot overcome it" (Jn 1:5); but there are times when it comes close. To join the labor of God in the world requires generosity and great-heartedness, those dispositions that open us to God's demanding invitation and promise joy in the struggle.

Discernment in the *Spiritual Exercises* does not end when the retreatant has made the decision about what to do with his or her life. It requires confirmation in the closing days of meditation on the passion and resurrection of Christ. Can these great hopes and plans stand in face of the scandal of the cross? Here the great paradigm of Christian life and service is brought to bear on our plans. If we trust God radically, then a new freedom and joy emerge. Whether our chosen path means a long life or a short one, sickness or health, success or failure does not finally matter since any of those experiences promises to be an opportunity to be a companion of Jesus in his struggle to free the world.[32] If this freedom increases over the months and years that follow the retreat, the life decision made in the retreat will be confirmed pragmatically.

This radical freedom should reinterpret the traditional notion of Jesuit obedience. The Jesuit on mission is not an automaton who has been programmed by his superior. He should be flexible and discerning in the situation, looking for the traces of God's working in all things. Almost every directive in the Jesuit *Constitutions*

38

presupposes the qualification, "keeping always in view the greater service of God and the universal good."[33] The Jesuit on the scene had to be obedient to the possibilities in the situation that God made evident which the superior could not have foreseen.

Ignatius never wanted his companions to be slowed down by hours of mental prayer. Rather than seeking contact with God on the sidelines, he wanted them to find it in the midst of action. In preaching, teaching, setting up institutions, caring for the poor and sick, friendship and rest, they should find the same relish or "devotion" they experience in their best moments of prayer. They need contemplation to attune their hearts to discern God in action; they need action to keep their contemplation honest and grounded in the desire for God's greater glory.

I think Jonathan Edwards and William James could understand this mysticism of service. If Jesuits had their hearts set on promoting the greater glory of God, their pragmatism would have clear direction, freedom, and joy. It would be a strenuous life because they were to seek Christ where he was laboring most intensely in the world.

The last word belongs to Charles Sanders Peirce, the first pragmatist. He could understand the connection between Jesuit pragmatism and the affective commitment to "the greater glory of God." For him, logic was subordinate to ethics, which was in turn subordinate to aesthetics. The ultimate foundations of truth and action are given in a disclosure of transcendent goodness and beauty.[34] Put more concisely, Ignatian discernment attunes the heart to recognize the beauty of the Lord who labors alongside us in all things, and that fact more than anything sets our moral discernment on the right track.

Postscript

What sort of moral theology would this blend of pragmatism and Ignatian spirituality produce? What would a Christian ethics look like if it were actually experiential, practical, emotionally charged, and transformative? Certainly it would be different from that which most of us were raised on and studied. It would center on conversion as the prerequisite for appreciating Christian values and norms. It would put rules at the service of the task of reconstruction of the world and building human community. It would probably claim less certitude for universal norms and would look to the actual results of practices to see whether they are enhancing the quality of life in a particular culture. It would rediscover the role of liturgy, prayer, and Scripture in shaping the imagination and affections of Christians to discern the appropriate responses to their own unique situations. The community would be a community of moral discourse and challenge that worked together to apply the story of Jesus to new problems.

As Mark Twain said, "History doesn't repeat itself, but it does rhyme." An American pragmatic moral theology would help us catch that rhyme.

Notes

¹ See Albert R. Jonsen and Stephen Toulmin, *The Abuse of Casuistry: A History of Moral Reasoning* (Berkeley: University of California, 1988), chapter 12.

² Obviously, this religious foundation plays a greater part in the writings of Jonathan Edwards, Horace Bushnell, Charles Sanders Peirce, Josiah Royce and H. Richard Niebuhr than in the best known pragmatists. A strong case could be made, however, that William James located the moral life within the foundation of a religious response, albeit in nontraditional terms. Dewey had little use for organized religion after his early thirties, but nevertheless indicates a universal scope in which moral action fits as part to whole. See William James, *Pragmatism: A New Name for Some Old Ways of Thinking* (Cambridge: Harvard University Press, 1975), lecture 8, "Pragmatism and Religion"; and Dewey's *Art as Experience* (New York: Putnam's Sons, 1958) 28-29, 129, 195, and *A Common Faith* (New Haven: Yale University Press, 1971).

³ Jonathan Edwards, *Religious Affections*, John E. Smith, ed. (New Haven: Yale University Press, 1959).

⁴ Ibid., 272.

⁵ Ibid., 281.

⁶ Ignatius of Loyola, *The Spiritual Exercises*, Elder Mullan, S.J., trans., in David L. Fleming, S.J., *The Spiritual Exercises of St. Ignatius: A Literal Translation and A Contemporary Reading* (St. Louis: Institute of

Jesuit Sources, 1978) para 2, p. 6; also para 76, p. 50.

[7] Edwards, *Affections*, 120. James strongly emphasizes this American theme that all judgment, even the most abstract, is based on felt experience: "The only answer can be that he will recognize its rationality as he recognizes everything else, by certain subjective marks with which it affects him. . . . A strong feeling of ease, peace, rest, is one of them. The transition from a state of puzzle and perplexity to rational apprehension is full of lively relief and pleasure . . . the absence of any feeling of irrationality . . . This feeling of the sufficiency of the present moment, of its absoluteness--this absence of all need to explain it, account for it, or justify it--is what I call the Sentiment of Rationality." *The Will to Believe and Other Essays in Popular Philosophy* (Cambridge: Harvard University Press, 1979), 57-58.

[8] William James, *The Principles of Psychology* (Cambridge: Harvard University Press, 1983), 1265.

[9] Ibid., 2767-77.

[10] See *Exercises*, "Three Times for Making, In Any One of Them, A Sound and Good Election," para 175-88, pp. 106-12. See Karl Rahner, *The Dynamic Element in the Church* (New York: Herder and Herder, 1964), chapter 3, "The Logic of Concrete Knowledge in Ignatius Loyola." An interesting comparison could be made with James's three criteria for judging the value of religious opinions and experiences: "*Immediate luminousness*, in short *philosophical reasonableness*, and *moral helpfulness* are the only available criteria." James, *The Varieties of Religious Experience* (Cambridge: Harvard University Press, 1975), 23.

[11] John Dewey, *Human Nature and Conduct: An Introduction to Social Psychology* (New York: Random House, 1957), 192. "We will experience some objects as welcome . . . Other objects rasp . . . they are tiresome, hateful, unwelcome . . . in no other way than as a bore who prolongs his visit, a dun we can't pay, or a pestiferous mosquito who goes on buzzing." Ibid., 200-201.

[12] One can trace the origins of the American insistence on the practical nature of truth and meaning to Edwards. The final and most important sign of religious experience is "Gracious and holy affections [that] have their exercise and fruit in Christian practice." He argues that every other sign means nothing unless it comes in a life of transformed practice. *Religious Affections*, 383. James and Dewey detached this test from the Puritan theology that justified it for Edwards.

[13] Ibid., 101. John Dewey locates the source of the affections in the qualities of the situation that they grasp. These qualities are the basis of

reflections and action because they form "the background, the point of departure, and the regulative principle of all thinking." John Dewey, *Philosophy and Civilization* (New York: Capricorn Books, 1963), 16.

¹⁴ Ibid., 95. This statement is the central thesis which the rest of his treatise demonstrates.

¹⁵ "They who condemn high affections in others are certainly not likely to have high affections themselves. And let it be considered, that they who have but little religious affection, have certainly but little religion." Ibid., 121.

¹⁶ "That which men love, they desire to have and to be united to, and possessed of. That beauty which men delight in, they desire to be adorned with. Those acts which men delight in, they necessarily incline to do." Ibid., 394. On the relation of particular values to the beauty of God, see Edwards, *The Nature of True Virtue in Ethical Writings*, Paul Ramsey, ed. (New Haven: Yale University Press, 1989).

¹⁷ E. Edward Kinerk, S.J. states Ignatius's four overlapping presuppositions about desires. "All desires are real experiences, but not all desires are equally authentic. . . . Our authentic desires are vocational. . . . The more authentic our desires, the more they move us to glorify God. . . . Authentic desires are always in some way public." "Eliciting Great Desires: Their Place in the Spirituality of the Society of Jesus," *Studies in the Spirituality of Jesuits* 16/5 (1984). See also Wilkie Au, S.J., *By Way of the Heart: Toward a Holistic Christian Spirituality* (New York: Paulist, 1989), chapter 3.

¹⁸ Ignatius, *Exercises*, para 1, p. 4. The aim of the *Exercises* is "to conquer oneself and regulate one's life without determining oneself through any tendency that is disordered." Ibid., para 21, p. 20.

¹⁹ Ibid. Rules for the Discernment of Spirits for the first sort are found in the *Exercises*, para 314-27; the second set of rules in para 328-36. Michael J. Buckley, S.J. writes that Ignatius brings together the three sources of spiritual guidance that have usually been kept apart in the history of religions: ideas, emotions, and experiences of various spirits. "Rules for the Discernment of Spirits," *The Way*, Supplement 20 (1973), 17-37.

²⁰ See the meditation on the Call of the King that stands at the threshold of the rest of the *Exercises* (paras. 91-98, pp. 64-68).

²¹ Edwards, *Affections*, 344-45.

²² See Josiah Royce, *The Problem of Christianity*, part 1, "The Christian Doctrine of Life" (Chicago: University of Chicago Press, 1968).

²³ See H. Richard Niebuhr, *The Meaning of Revelation* (New York: Macmillan, 1960), chapter 2, "The Story of Our Life." Niebuhr drew on

Jonathan Edwards, Josiah Royce, and Dewey's disciple, George Herbert Mead in shaping his responsibility ethics. Niebuhr describes how the story of Christ functions as a paradigm of responsibility. The responsible Christian "tests the spirits to see if among all the forces that move within him, his societies, the human mind itself, there be a healing, a knowing, a whole-making spirit, a Holy Spirit. And he can do so only with the aid of the image, the symbol of Christ. 'Is there a Christ-like spirit here?'" H.R. Niebuhr, *The Responsible Self: An Essay in Christian Moral Philosophy* (New York: Harper & Row, 1963), 155.

[24] Ignatius always places discernment in the context of conversation with others. This interpersonal search for the appropriate action often seems missing in James and Dewey. For Ignatius other people, whether pope, superior, retreat director, or the Jesuit's co-workers, form a public test of private inspiration. The institutional church also served as a public test of personal discernment. Ignatius expected the Spirit of charismatic inspiration to agree with the public doctrines of the church. This does not rule out prophetic challenge to authority figures, as the history of Ignatius with various popes and bishops makes clear. Dewey's reliance on democratic processes to test out values reflects a similar concern for a public dimension to inquiry. See his *Philosophy and Civilization* (New York: Capricorn Books, 1963).

[25] "The deepest thing in our nature is . . . this dumb region of the heart in which we dwell alone with our willingnesses and unwillingnesses, our faiths and fears. . . .in these crepuscular depths of personality the sources of all our outer deeds and decisions take their rise. Here is our deepest organ of communication with the nature of things; and compared with these concrete movements of our soul all abstract statements and scientific arguments . . . sound to us like mere chatterings of the teeth." William James, *The Will to Believe and Other Essays in Popular Philosophy* (Cambridge: Harvard University Press, 1979), 55.

[26] See Howard M. Feinstein, *Becoming William James* (Ithaca, N.Y.: Cornell University, 1984), especially chapter 18.

[27] "... and even though one be quite free from melancholy one's self, there is no doubt that healthy-mindedness is inadequate as a philosophical doctrine, because the evil facts which it refuses positively to account for are a genuine portion of reality; and they may after all be the best key to life's significance and possibly only openers of our eyes to the deepest levels of truth." *Varieties*, 136. "Morality pure and simple accepts the law of the whole which it finds reigning, so far as to acknowledge and obey it, but it may obey it with the heaviest and coldest heart, and never cease to feel it as a yoke. But for religion, in its strong and fully developed

43

manifestations, the service of the highest is never felt as a yoke. Dull submission is left behind, and a mood of welcome, which may fill any place on the scale between cheerful serenity and enthusiastic gladness, has taken its place." James, *Varieties*, 41. In this work James's description of the relation between religion and morality closely resembles the standard Reformation account wherein a weary morality ultimately surrenders to the gracious gift of religious faith which renews the moral life with new spirit, energy, and scope. Whether this account reflects his own position or the common view of his sources of religious experiences, which were largely Protestant, is difficult to determine.

[28] James, *Pragmatism*, 36.

[29] See "The Moral Philosopher and the Moral Life," in *Will to Believe*, 146-50.

[30] James, *Will to Believe*, 55.

[31] Ibid.

[32] See Ignatius, *Exercises*, on the three kinds of humility: paras. 165-67, p. 100.

[33] Ignatius of Loyola, *The Constitutions of the Society of Jesus*, trans. with an introduction and commentary by George E. Ganss, S.J. (St. Louis, Mo.: Institute of Jesuit Sources, 1970), para. 650, p. 283. See also the pragmatic flexibility evident in his criteria for choosing ministries, in para. 623, pp. 275-76.

[34] Charles Sanders Peirce, *Collected Papers of Charles Sanders Peirce*, Charles Hartshorne and Paul Weiss, eds. (Cambridge, Mass.: Belknap, 1935), 1.611, 1.615, 5.126, 5.551.

Jeffrey L. Klaiber, S.J.

The Pursuit of Utopia: Religion and Politics in Latin America

Jeffrey L. Klaiber, S.J. is Associate Professor of History at the
Catholic University of Peru in Lima.

L atin America is a continent of believers. The popular classes of Latin America may not necessarily belong to the "believer's church" of which the Protestant reformers spoke, but they have always believed in religion as the ultimate and final statement on life, society, and history. The belief that a more just and fraternal society is possible and the hope that it will come to pass have been two fundamental moving forces in the world view of Latin America's popular classes since the sixteenth century. Indeed, many of the Europeans who formed part of the dominant cultural elite were themselves inspired by the belief that the New World was a privileged place where Utopia or Utopias could be brought about. But the hope or dream of entering the Promised Land of justice and freedom lived on long after the sixteenth century and resurfaced from time to time throughout the next four centuries in different forms and movements. Liberation is but one of its latest manifestations. The pursuit of "Utopia" is therefore a central theme in Latin America's history. Although many Christians have fought and died to bring about this just and fraternal society, it seems fitting, as we are about to commemorate the first anniversary of the martyrs of El Salvador (November 16), to make special mention of the Jesuits' role in this story.

Karl Mannheim's notions of "ideology" and "Utopia" help to throw light on the ways in which religion and politics are related in Latin American history. Mannheim defined ideology largely in the Marxist sense as a set of ideas or attitudes which tend to legitimize and bolster up the status quo. By way of contrast, "Utopia" consists in beliefs and dreams which envision a new and better society and which therefore challenge the status quo.[1] Religion in Latin America was both ideology and Utopia from the very beginning. The Spanish conquerors used both the sword and the cross to impose a new order on the Indians and black slaves. But the missionaries and other humanists also presented Christianity as Utopia and opposed the use of Christian symbols to justify the destruction of entire civilizations and to violate human rights.

Many of the exponents of utopian Christianity are well known and have lived on as symbols of what was best in Latin America's colonial history. The Franciscan missionaries in New Spain were

47

moved fundamentally by a utopian and apocalyptic view of society. Although messianic or apocalyptic notions were not new, they acquired peculiar nuances when applied to the New World. Jerónimo de Mendieta, the sixteenth century Franciscan missionary, used the parable of the wedding feast in Saint Luke (Chapter 14) to explain the unique mission of the friars in Mexico. The Spanish king was God's messenger sent to call the guests to the feast. But the first two groups invited, the Jews and the Moors, did not accept the invitation. Therefore, the call went out to "the poor, the weak, the blind and the lame" on the highways, who in this case turned out to be the Indians of the New World.[2] For Mendieta, the Franciscans and the Indians were called to forge together a kingdom of peace and brotherly love, far removed from the intrigues and sordid politics of the courts of Europe.

But Mendieta was not the only believer in Utopia. Vasco de Quiroga (1470-1565), the Spanish layman who went to Mexico as a member of the second Audiencia and later became bishop of Michoacán, founded one of the first consciously conceived utopian experiments in the New World, the "Hospitals of Santa Fe" in Mexico and in Michoacán. "Tata" Vasco, as he was known affectionately by the Indians, literally modeled his republic of the hospitals for poor and sick Indians on the Utopia of Thomas More.[3] Bartolomé de las Casas also founded an experimental community for Indians, which was much less successful.

That Europeans entertained utopian expectations with respect to the New World is well known. Less well known is the fact that the newly Christianized Indians and Blacks from the very beginning also gave rise to their own utopian projections. In Peru around the beginning of the seventeenth century, Felipe Huamán Poma de Ayala, a Christian Indian, wrote one of the most famous chronicles of colonial society. Felipe had served as an interpreter and secretary to government and church officials and during a period of thirty years collected data on conditions in Peru. His chronicle, famous for some four hundred drawings which depict daily life in Peru before and after the conquest, was addressed to King Philip III. The author not only described conditions in Peru but also called for sweeping reform in both society and the Church.

What is most intriguing is his frequent statement that the Peruvians were better off physically and morally before the conquest and evangelization. The Indians before the conquest, claimed Huamán Poma, did not steal, lie, or fight among themselves to acquire gold or silver. Even though they were idolaters, he declared, they practiced the works of mercy and kept the commandments better than the Spanish Christians did in his day.[4]

The Indian chronicler also took the missionaries to task for not living up to their mission. He condemned the priests in the *doctrines* (Indian parishes) who mistreated their wards. They are "given to anger and [act like] absolute lords and they are very arrogant."[5] By way of exception he praised the Franciscans, hermits, and the Jesuits. He described the latter as "very holy men, very learned and good preachers."[6] Finally, he made a political proposal, which he carefully couched in respectful and even naive terms: that Peru be allowed to govern itself within a Christian world empire under the king in Spain:

> . . . the entire world is under God, and just as Castille is of the Spaniards and the Indies are of the Indians and Guinea (Africa) is of the blacks, so each one is the rightful owner of their kingdom . . . not by decree of the king, but by God and by justice . . .[7]

Felipe, with the subversive self-deprecation characteristic of the conquered, drew a picture of himself, on bended knee, presenting his great reform plan to the king himself. Clearly, for Huamán Poma and other Indian and mestizo authors, Utopia was to be a Christian society, but based upon the native Indian culture and freed of Spanish domination.

But protest and religious belief manifested itself not only in privileged Indians or mestizos who could read or write. Popular religiosity, long dismissed as a fatalistic and deformed Catholicism, very often represented a protest against the status quo. The legends that shroud the history of two of the most famous devotions in Latin America not only shed light on how evangelization really occurred in most parts of Latin America, but they also contain elements of resistance, protest, and self-assertion that form a part of popular religiosity. As is well known, according to the legend of Guadalupe,

Bishop Zumarraga dismissed Juan Diego's claim to have seen the Virgin of the Spanish God on the hill called Tepeyac outside Mexico City. But Juan Diego, a peasant, persisted, and finally presented the bishop with a miracle, roses gathered on that desert hill wrapped in his mantle, and with the image of the Lady imprinted on it. The bishop backed down and permitted a small chapel to be built on the site. From that point on, the Virgin of Guadalupe became the central focus of the evangelization of Mexico. Indeed, within time she became a symbol of Mexico itself. When Miguel Hidalgo summoned the Indians to follow him in 1810, it was under the banner of the Virgin of Guadalupe. In the contest between Juan Diego and the bishop, Juan Diego won: the Virgin he created and represented became the symbol of Indian and popular Catholicism.

In Peru in 1651 a devastating earthquake nearly leveled the city of Lima. It was the month of October when most earthquakes, at least according to popular lore, occur. A black slave had previously painted the image of the crucified Christ on the wall of a room where the slaves met. The wall survived the earthquake. A Spanish gentleman began to care for the image and soon he was cured of a cancerous tumor. The image and the devotion that grew up around it soon became known as the "Lord of Miracles." According to popular legend (but quite possibly true), the archbishop of Lima, wishing to do away with a suspicious devotion, ordered the image to be destroyed. The soldiers sent to do the job reported that mysterious forces held them back from completing their mission. The archbishop grudgingly gave in. The black slaves began taking an image of the painting out in procession each year. The procession grew in popularity and by the eighteenth century it was the biggest in Lima. It is now one of the biggest processions in the entire Catholic world. During the three days in which the procession is held, hundreds of thousands of Peruvians pay their respects to the Lord of Miracles. The confraternity in charge of the procession is made up largely of Lima's mestizo, mulatto, and black population. This same story, of the Virgin of Guadalupe and the Lord of Miracles, was repeated in different places and contexts throughout Latin America, but the basic elements are almost always the same: the people accepted Catholicism, but on their terms. They infused the symbols of conquest with their own meanings and nuances. Popular religiosity does not refer merely to the lower-class nature of many of these devotions, but to the fact that they are creations of the people.

The tenacity, the strength, and the widespread acceptance of these popular devotions were not due necessarily or even primarily to the efforts of the missionaries, although they did foster them, but fundamentally to the fact that they represented a symbolic counterculture with which the lower classes identified. Popular religiosity became therefore the key symbolic means by which most lower-class Latin Americans coped with the harshness of colonial exploitation: it brought them consolation and the strength to go on believing in God and final justice for close to five centuries.

The utopian phase of evangelization ended in Latin America just as Huamán Poma took pen in hand to project his own Utopia. By the end of the sixteenth century a narrow nationalism replaced the more open Renaissance-infused humanism of Charles V. As Spain closed its doors to the rest of Europe in the face of the threat of Protestantism, it also tightened its ideological grip on its New World inhabitants. Rigid orthodoxy replaced the initially tolerant and creative missiology of the first missionaries.

But Utopia flourished beyond the confines of "civilization"--in the Franciscan and Jesuit missions in the jungles and deserts of all Latin America and a good part of North America. These two great missionary orders established hundreds of missions on the periphery of the empire--in California, Arizona, Texas, the jungles of eastern Bolivia, Paraguay, and Brazil. The ideal of Bartolomé de las Casas of a peaceful evangelization was really achieved in these remote areas. Although the basic vision that inspired the founding of these missions was the same, to carve out little patches of Christian civilization uncontaminated by civilized and sinful Europeans, there were striking differences between the two systems. The Franciscan mission, with its emphasis on simplicity and poverty, reflected more the ideal of the medieval monastery-Utopia of Campanella's *The City of the Sun.* But the Jesuits' missions very clearly reflected the ideal of the Renaissance secular Utopia as conceived by Thomas More. Their missions, and especially the reductions of Paraguay, were characterized by their economic creativity, their emphasis on culture, music, and learning, as well as on spiritual values. And who but the Jesuits would think of arming their Indians and training them to fight for themselves? The great Jesuit experiment of Paraguay is too well known to retell in detail here. What is important is to emphasize the missions as the connecting links between the utopian dreams and experiments of the sixteenth century and those of the eighteenth century.

The Jesuits who went to Paraguay had previously established a model Indian community in Juli by the shores of Lake Titicaca. The first Paraguay missions were founded in 1607. The thirty towns in what are now present-day Paraguay, Argentina, Brazil, and Uruguay were complemented by another thirty towns in eastern Bolivia. The so-called "Jesuit Republic" of Paraguay and Bolivia may have gathered together around 300,000 Indians at the height of the experiment. When Charles III expelled the Society of Jesus from Spanish America in 1767, the Paraguay missions were famous in Europe. Many of the ideologues of the French Revolution, including Voltaire, saw that New World society as a possible model for a reformed Europe. Candide, the innocent hero of Voltaire's novel, marvelled at the wonders of Paraguay (although he was not pleased with the presence of the Jesuits) and most of all at the kingdom of *El Dorado* which he discovered somewhere deep in the Peruvian jungle. It was largely the great Jesuit experiment of Paraguay that convinced Europeans once again that Utopias were possible.

But the memory of Paraguay lived on to influence future Latin American intellectuals as well. Writing in 1928, Jose Carlos Mariátegui, the founder of Marxism in Peru, had nothing but praise for the Jesuits in Juli and in Paraguay:

> Only the Jesuits, with their systematic positivism, showed in Peru, as in other countries of America, some aptitude for economic creation. The latifundia assigned to them prospered and traces of their organization still survive. Remembering how skillfully the Jesuits in Paraguay made use of the native's natural

inclination to communal work, it is not surprising that this congregation of the sons of Saint Ignatius of Loyola . . . created centers of work and production on Peruvian soil, while nobles, lawyers and priests enjoyed a luxurious and worldly life in Lima.[8]

Admirable though their economic creativity may have been, that was not the driving force behind the missions. As Cunninghame Graham, author of *A Vanished Arcadia* (1901), stated: "The Jesuits did not conduct the missions after the fashion of a business concern, but rather as the rulers of some utopia--those foolish beings who think happiness is preferable to wealth."[9] The great heroes of the missions--Nobrega, Anchieta, and Antonio de Vieira in Brazil, Antonio Ruiz de Montoya and Roque González in Paraguay--were Utopia-builders: practical men, yet visionaries driven by love and by faith.

By the eighteenth century the Spanish American colonies had grown to become sophisticated multiracial societies, and Bourbon absolutism reached its zenith. But signs of discontent abounded and pointed to a major struggle ahead. The greatest revolution in colonial Peru, and indeed in all of South America, was sparked in 1780 by Tupac Amaru, an Indian leader who unleashed centuries of pent-up resentment against the many abuses that the Indians had endured. Born in 1740 in a town south of Cuzco, Joseph Gabriel Condorcanqui was a descendant of the daughter of Tupac Amaru I, the last Inca, who was beheaded by the Viceroy Francisco Toledo in Cuzco in 1572. As the son of a *cacique* (chieftain), he received a formal education far surpassing that of an ordinary Indian. He was taught how to read and write by priests who lived near his village, and at the age of ten he was sent to study with the Jesuits at San Francisco Borja, the school they ran for the sons of *caciques* and Inca nobility in Cuzco. During the five or six years that he studied with the Jesuits, Joseph Gabriel learned the basics of Christian doctrine, reading, writing, geography, and all other subjects that the son of a Spaniard or creole would learn. In 1760 he married Micaela Bastida, also of Indian-white blood.

By the decade of the 1770s he had become a prosperous businessman who transported goods by means of mules across the southern highlands. He had also become a conspirator planning to disrupt Spain's dominion in Peru. On November 10, 1780, in the presence of several thousand Indians he lynched the king's official in the small town of Tungasuca, to the south of Cuzco. He was promptly declared a public criminal by the viceroy, and the bishop of Cuzco excommunicated him and all his followers. His revolution swept across southern Peru and spread to Bolivia. He now bore the title of "Tupac Amaru II" to indicate that he considered himself the rightful successor to the Incas. Although he pretended that he was acting under the king's orders, so as not to challenge the myth of kingship too openly, in fact he was hailed as a king everywhere he went. In his triumphal march through the towns and countryside he decreed the end to black slavery and all forms of abuses to which the Indians were subjected. He invited the creoles and sympathetic Whites to join him in his crusade. Although excommunicated, he presented himself in public with all the symbols of a Christian monarch. He entered every town preceded by the cross and candles and had masses of thanksgiving celebrated for his victories. He published edicts forbidding priests to be harmed, even those who condemned his movement. His wife, Micaela Bastidas, maintained regular correspondence with priests who were sympathetic to the revolution.

The king sent over General José Antonio Areche with a force of several thousand professional soldiers to put down the rebellion and restore order in Peru. Areche wrote a public letter to Tupac Amaru in which he denounced him as a "traitor to the king" and an "apostate" who was leading the Indians back into idolatrous ways. Areche's letter motivated Tupac Amaru to write his own public letter, dated March 5, 1781. In it Tupac Amaru claimed, somewhat unconvincingly, that he was really loyal to the king, who really was not aware of the terrible abuses being committed in Peru. But his defense of his Christian beliefs are much more convincing. He cited the Bible to compare himself with David and Moses:

> A humble youth with a rod and a slingshot, and a country
> shepherd, by divine providence, freed the unhappy people of
> Israel from the power of Goliath and the Pharaoh; the reason for

their liberation was that the tears of those poor captives became cries for compassion and justice which reached Heaven, so that they were able to leave behind their martyrdom and torments in order to find their way to the Land of Promise ... but we unhappy Indians, with more cries and tears than theirs, after so many centuries have not found such divine consolation . . .[10]

The biblical comparison between Tupac Amaru and Old Testament figures was also made by a priest in a letter to Micaela Bastidas:

Just as God used David ... and elected Moses to save the people of Israel from Pharaoh's oppression, so, too, I suppose that he has made Joseph Gabriel Tupac Amaru an instrument for the correction of many evils and abuses . . .[11]

In his letter Tupac Amaru goes on to show that the real Christians in Peru are the Indians, not the king's officials. He refers to Nero and Attila the Hun in order to compare them with the king's officials:

For them (Nero and Attila) there is forgiveness, because they were infidels; but the *corregidores*, being baptized, belie their Christianity with their works, and they really seem more like atheists, Calvinists and Lutherans, because they are enemies of God and of man, idolaters of gold and silver . . .[12]

The Indian leader turned theologian went on to analyze the Ten Commandments to see who were the real Christians in Peru. After pointing out that the Indians under him practiced all the commandments and precepts of the church, Tupac Amaru ended with a rhetorical challenge to Areche: "Who are apostates to the faith, the Indians or the *corregidores*?. . ."[13]

The great rebellion ended in defeat. In May 1781, Tupac Amaru, his family and many of his followers were drawn and quartered in the public square of Cuzco. With the bloody repression to which thousands of Indians were subjected so too died the dream of a Christian Inca monarchy. The dream of a Christian Utopia carved out of native Latin American realities and based on the belief that Indians, Blacks, and Whites should live together in a new brotherhood, made its most dramatic manifestation in late colonial Latin America in Tupac Amaru's revolution. But the belief in an independent Latin America did not die: it lived on, ironically, in Tupac Amaru's mentors, the Jesuits, who had so obviously influenced him, and who after his defeat took up the torch of independence.

The Jesuits were exiled from Spanish America in 1767. From their exile in Europe many of them continued to foster the seeds of nationalism and to promote the cause of independence, making them the first creoles to take an open stand in favor of complete separation from Spain. One of the most famous of the exiled Jesuits was Francisco Clavijero, whose history of Mexico, written to refute erroneous notions of certain Europeans about America, served to enkindle pride in Mexicans about their country. But the most famous political activist of the exiled Jesuits was Juan Pablo Viscardo y Guzman, from Peru. Born near Arequipa in 1748, Juan Pablo entered the Jesuit novitiate in Cuzco in 1761. He was exiled, along with his younger brother, also a Jesuit, at the age of twenty. Like the other 2,200 exiled Jesuits from Spanish America, he never returned to his native land. In Tuscany where he was exiled, he became secularized in 1769. Nevertheless, he retained the status of a cleric with minor orders and frequently referred to himself as an ex-Jesuit. His career as a political propagandist for independence was very likely prompted by Tupac Amaru's revolt. In 1781 Viscardo y Guzman wrote a letter to the English consul in Livorno urging the British government to send aid to Tupac Amaru in his struggle against the Spanish. Although Tupac Amaru had actually been defeated when he wrote, the letter nevertheless served to reveal Viscardo's sympathies.

But Viscardo is most famous for his *Letter to the Spanish Americans* (meaning "creoles"), in which he urged his fellow Latin Americans to break with Spain and proclaim their independence. The letter, really a political pamphlet, can only be compared to Thomas Paine's *Common Sense* for its influence and propaganda impact. When Viscardo wrote it is not clear. He died in London (still pursuing his mission of urging the British to take action) in

1798. Before dying he left all his papers in the hands of his friend, Rufus King, the American minister to the English court. King lent the papers to General Francisco Miranda, a leading Venezuelan conspirator who was also one of Simón Bolívar's mentors. It was Miranda who had the letter translated from the original French and published in Spanish. The letter circulated rapidly throughout Spanish America: by the time of independence, creole conspirators from Caracas to Potosi had read it.

Like all well-written political propaganda, it captured the imagination and inspired people to belief. Viscardo relied heavily on the concept of the natural right of all peoples to forge their own nation. He pointed to the sufferings of the Indians, the injustices which the creoles endured, and the expulsion of the Jesuits as proof of Spanish despotism. He also singled out the struggle for independence of the English colonies in North America as an example to follow. In short, Viscardo was a political liberal imbued with the spirit of the age. But he was also a devout Catholic and, like most Latin Americans, he did not look to the French Revolution with its antireligiosity as a model. The Utopia of eighteenth century political liberalism found one of its best expressions in Viscardo's celebrated essay.

During the independence movement, the creole clergy took up the cause and in many cases they were the main instigators and leaders. Miguel Hidalgo y Costilla, who raised the banner of Guadalupe in Mexico in 1810, was captured and shot by the Inquisition. But the cause was kept alive by another priest, José María Morelos, who was also captured and killed. While the vast majority of the bishops, all of whom had been chosen by the king, condemned independence, the lower clergy defied threats of excommunication and exhorted fellow creoles and the Indians to join the side of patriotism. Ideology and Utopia vied with each other within the church as never before. By the end of the wars, liberal priests were hailed everywhere as patriots and founding fathers of the new nations. In the first constitutional assembly of Peru nearly half the elected delegates were priests, and the president of the assembly was Francisco de Luna Pizarro, a priest from Arequipa.

But Rome had the final word. Embroiled as Catholicism was in battles with liberals, Masons, and anticlericals in Europe, the pope looked dimly on liberalism in America and named conservative bishops to the vacant dioceses in the New World. They in turn weeded out the liberals in the church. By 1850 the Latin American church had turned ultramontane and politically conservative. Francisco Javier Mariátegui, a leading liberal and one of the founders of Freemasonry in Peru, lamented the passing of his priest friends with whom he had fought for independence. Writing in 1869, he exclaimed: "What I wouldn't give that the priests of today were like those of 1820 in wisdom, patriotism and virtue!"[14]

The nineteenth century was not the best of times for utopian dreams in Latin America. Military caudillos soon swept away the precarious democracies and by 1850 liberalism had become an ideology to justify capitalist expansion, usually at the expense of the Indians, Blacks, and other groups belonging to the lower classes. Indeed, according to many historians, the nineteenth century was the worst one for the Indians. The liberals discarded the old Spanish paternalism that had treated the Indians as minors, but which had also protected them from the white population. That protection was ended in the name of liberty and everywhere Indians lost their lands to expanding haciendas. New immigrants from Europe brought their racial prejudices with them. The dominant philosophy in political and intellectual circles in the latter part of the century was positivism, which was really another name for social Darwinism. The upper classes looked to England or the United States as their model for development and at the same time expressed disdain for the Indians, Blacks, and other racial mixtures in society. Although the Church continued to offer consolation to the lower classes, it had no social message which might have served as an alternative vision to liberalism or positivism.

Spiritualism and utopian expectations were enkindled anew, not by churchmen, but by leftists who spoke out against the status quo. Two figures stand out especially in this regard: José Carlos Mariátegui and Haya de la Torre, both Peruvians. Mariátegui was a devout Catholic as a youth, and he even won a prize for his sympathetic description of the Lord of Miracles procession in Lima, but after a visit to Italy in the early 1920s he returned to Peru with the aim of founding the first communist party there. Nevertheless, Mariátegui is famous in the history of the left in Latin America because he espoused the creation of a Latin American Marxism to be built upon local realities. His praise for the Jesuit missions, which we noted earlier, was motivated by more than dispassionate interest. Even though he claimed to be a Marxist, he never lost his nostalgia for religion (and his Italian wife and all his sons were and are practicing Catholics). He was the first Marxist in Latin America to discover a link between religion and revolution. He announced in an interview that very early in life "his soul had gone in search of God: and that in the process he had discovered his new 'faith.'"[15] On many other occasions he stated that without faith in some higher vision a person or a society will stagnate and lose the power to be creative. In his classic Marxist treatment of Peruvian history, he considered religion as one of the basic elements in Peruvian society. Religion was the basis of the Inca empire, and Catholicism was the legitimizing founding stone of colonial society. In some way or another the new socialist society of the future must be based on a religion to ground and sustain that new experience.[16]

In the twenties and thirties Victor Raul Haya de la Torre, founder of the Aprista Party, became the standard bearer of social reform in Peru and a spokesman for a united Latin America. In 1932 he was imprisoned and his party severely repressed. He and the other party leaders had harbored anticlerical sentiments as university students, like most other reformists in Latin America at that time. But unlike the other reformers, the experience of persecution led the Peruvian Apristas to seek a common language to express the collective sufferings of the movement's followers in terms which the popular classes would most readily understand. While the PRI (Partido Revolucionario Institucionalizado) of Mexico, a party very similar to the Peruvian APRA, persecuted Catholics, Apristas openly appealed to the religious sentiment of their Catholic constituents to win support for their cause. On one dramatic occasion in 1933, Haya addressed the party faithful to pay tribute to the memory of several hundred Apristas who had been executed by the dictator Sánchez Cerro. He compared the party to the crucified Christ and exhorted

59

his followers to prepare for martyrdom.[17] Another Aprista leader died with these words: "Only God will save my soul and only APRA will save Peru!"[18]

The originality of these two political figures lay in their capacity to look beyond the dogmatic blinds of Marxism and liberalism and discover positive values in popular Christianity. By so doing they also gave new meaning to popular religious symbols. Mariátegui the Marxist praised belief in unseen kingdoms to come as a necessary quality for a revolutionary, and Haya de la Torre identified social reform with popular religious symbols. Neither one saw religious belief as an obstacle to fighting for social justice. In fact, both were convinced that the Indians, peasants, and workers of Peru and the rest of Latin America wished to do just that: believe in God and believe in social reform or revolution at the same time.

The revolt of Cristeros in Mexico in the twenties confirmed this intuition: the peasants who took up arms and cried "Long live Christ the King!" stood for both traditional values and social justice. They did not oppose the revolution, but rather the "socialist millionaires" under Plutarco Calles who lived off corruption while denying them the right to practice their religion as they always had.

Mariátegui died in 1930, and under pressure from Stalin, the Communist Party which he founded, as well as all other communist parties throughout Latin America, shunned Mariátegui's ideas and became tools of Soviet communism. Haya de la Torre in his later years followed a more conservative course and by the seventies he was warning young priests against the dangers of "Marxist infiltration" in the Church. For awhile Fidel Castro took up the torch of Utopia as did other revolutionary movements in their time. But the Cuban experience was limited because it lacked recourse to transcendental symbols. This was one of the basic differences between the Nicaraguan revolution and the Cuban: in Nicaragua, religion and the explicit use of Christian symbols to legitimize revolution played a significant role in the overthrow of Somoza.

Shortly after the Cuban revolution, Utopia surfaced in a most unlikely place, and on a much vaster scale, embracing all of Latin America and beyond, in the very institution that had first preached the idea in the sixteenth century: the Catholic Church. When the bishops of Latin America solemnly committed the Church to support the cause of justice and peace by implementing fundamental structural change in society, and later on at Puebla when they called upon Christians to "opt preferentially for the poor," they dramatically introduced an entire new chapter in the history of Christianity. The notion of a theology of liberation caught the imagination of Christians (Catholics and Protestants) and secular humanists everywhere. In the face of repressive dictatorships and military regimes in Nicaragua, Brazil, Argentina, El Salvador, Chile, Paraguay, Bolivia--and in the nominal democracies in the rest of Latin America--bishops, priests, religious women, and lay leaders became the new spokespersons for social change and the new prophets for denouncing violations of human rights. An unlikely class of people became folk heroes: bishops and theologians. Pedro Casaldáliga in the jungles of Brazil, Aloisio Lorscheider in Fortaleza, Leonidas Proaño in Riobamba, Helder Cámara in Recife, Silva Henríquez in Santiago were a few of the many bishops of Latin America who were popularly acclaimed as prophets in their own day. Some became martyrs: Oscar Romero in El Salvador and Enrique Angelelli in Argentina. Gustavo Gutiérrez, Leonard Boff, and other theologians command a following of admirers among intellectuals and the very poor in Latin America. Religious women too, many of whom have suffered martyrdom, have become heroines in the eyes of the popular classes.

Critics of the progressive church in Latin America have welcomed the recent conservative turn in the Catholic world as a way to curb what they considered to be unruly excesses or naive dabbling in Marxism. But they fail to understand the depth and force of religious sentiment that gave rise to the progressive church. The popularity of liberation theology, for example, is not due to a momentary fascination with a new idea, but to the fact that it gave expression to a deeply felt sentiment that had always been there, waiting to be tapped. Indeed, one of the valid criticisms of liberation theology, as Juan Luis Segundo pointed out in a talk on "The Shift within Latin American Theology,"[19] was that in the beginning the theologians relied too much on Marxism in the belief that this was a necessary vehicle by which to dialogue with politi-

61

cized Latin Americans. In the face of persecution, however, and in their efforts to reach out to the poor, they discovered what is the central theme of this paper: that there has always been a "liberation theology," in one way or another, embedded in the popular religiosity of the poor of Latin America. It was not necessary to have recourse to European or North American ideologies to talk to the people. It was sufficient to speak to them in terms of their own religious faith, naturally, of course, enriched with insights drawn from the social sciences, including Marxism, in order to communicate on a level that they would both understand and accept.

From Huamán Poma in sixteenth century Peru to Tupac Amaru in the eighteenth century to Oscar Romero in the twentieth, there is a connecting link that binds them together: they were Christians who denounced injustices and violence done against other human beings because they believed in a world in which men and women could live in peace, sharing the good things of life among themselves, and treating each other as brothers and sisters. They were "Utopians" because they did not accept the narrow and unforgiving status quo imposed by "ideology." The form and shape of Utopia may change from age to age, just as ideology may change. As Mannheim noted, "the road of history leads from one topia over a utopia to the next topia, etc."[20] But the root cause of the antagonism remains the same: Utopia uplifts and dignifies because one reaches out to God in efforts to build the City of God on earth; but ideology is the closing of the mind to God and to others in the effort to impose a fixed formula on others, usually to the benefit of a few. Utopians are always on the road to freedom; ideologists are always making new rules to curb freedom.

The story of the Jesuit missions in Paraguay was really a case study of Utopia versus ideology. But that same story is being repeated in Latin America (indeed, in the entire Third World) on a much greater scale-- between those who would construct a peaceable society through solidarity and sharing and those who would impose order from above.

One year ago, on November 16, 1989, six Jesuits and two women were murdered in El Salvador by persons who were blind both to God and to others. But for the millions of Latin Americans who believe in the kingdom of truth, justice, and love, the killing of those eight and of the many other Christians who have died for the same cause will serve only to inspire them to believe even more. They will cherish all the more the memory of those who were called to the Wedding Feast before them.

Notes

[1] Karl Mannheim, *Ideology and Utopia: an Introduction to the Sociology of Knowledge* (New York: Harcourt, Brace and World, Inc., 1968). See especially pages 173-75 for an application of the concepts of "ideology" and "Utopia" to medieval Christianity.

[2] Jéronimo de Mendieta, *Historia eclesiástica indiana* (Madrid: Biblioteca de Autores Españoles, 1973), vol. 260, 17-19. See also John Leddy Phelan, *The Millennial Kingdom of the Franciscans in the New World* (Berkeley: University of California Press, 1956) and Delno C. West, "Medieval Ideas of Apocalyptic Mission and the Early Franciscans in Mexico," *The Americas* 45, no. 3 (January 1989): 293-313.

[3] Silvio Zavala, *La Utopía de Tomás Moro en la Nueva España* (Mexico: J. Porrúa e hijos, 1937).

[4] *Nueva crónica y buen gobierno de Felipe Huamán Poma de Ayala*, edition and prologue by Franklin Pease (Caracas: Biblioteca de Ayacucho, 1980), vol. 1, 42, 49; vol. 2, 298.

[5] Ibid., vol. 2, 10.

[6] Ibid., vol. 2, 72, 74.

[7] Ibid., vol. 2, 302.

[8] José Carlos Mariátegui, *Seven Interpretive Essays on Peruvian Reality*, trans. Marjory Urguidi (Austin: University of Texas Press, 1971), 5.

[9] Philip Caraman, *The Lost Paradise: The Jesuit Republic in South America* (New York: The Seabury Press, 1976), 130.

[10] Jeffrey Klaiber, "Religión y justicia en Tupac Amaru," *Allpanchis* 16, no. 19 (Cuzco, 1982), 179.

[11] Ibid., 180.

[12] Ibid., 179.

[13] Ibid., 181.

[14] Jeffrey Klaiber, *La Iglesia en el Perú* (Lima: Pontificia Universidad Católica, 1988), 94.

[15] Jeffrey Klaiber, *Religion and Revolution in Peru, 1824-1976* (Notre Dame, Ind.: University of Notre Dame Press, 1977), 93.

[16] Ibid., 106, 113.

[17] Ibid., 144-50.

[18] Ibid., 151-52.

[19] Cited in Jeffrey Klaiber, "Prophets and Populists: Liberation Theology, 1968-1988," *The Americas* 46 (July 1989), 7-8.

[20] Mannheim, 178.

Diana L. Hayes

Church and Culture: A Black Catholic Womanist Perspective

Diana L. Hayes is Assistant Professor of Theology at Georgetown University.

I daresay that this presentation will be somewhat different from those that have preceded it in this lecture series. Perhaps that is because I am unlike any of the speakers who have participated in this series to date. For I am not nor ever have been nor ever plan to be a Jesuit, nor am I male, nor am I of European descent--at least not so's you could tell.

I am a black woman; I am a lay black female celibate Catholic theologian--an affirmative action dream. I am a convert to Catholicism from one of the historically black Protestant churches. My presence in the Catholic Church and my participation in its life have continually been challenged, by Catholic and Protestant alike, black and white, who see me as a contradiction, an anomaly, and who, thereby, challenge my authenticity. I do not belong; my people do not belong in the Roman Catholic Church. What am I doing here?

This question has come back to me time and time again since I was asked to participate in this lecture series. Why, in heaven's name, did he ask me? After a great deal of reflection, especially as the date rapidly approached, over what I would say and what, if anything, it would have to do with Ignatius of Loyola, I slowly began to realize that, quite possibly, it was "in heaven's name" that I was being asked to speak: to speak in the name of the many voiceless ones, women of all races, men and women of the "marginalized" races in our society in this nation. For in this anniversary year of the founding of the Society of Jesus and the approaching five hundredth anniversary of the arrival of Europeans onto the shores of this land, for good and for ill, there are still marginalized peoples, "voiceless ones," whose concerns too often are ignored because they are too often invisible and misunderstood.

Thus, I would like to speak to you about coming to voice, about discerning the movement of the Spirit within yourself, which is the central focus of Ignatius's *Spiritual Exercises*. But I would like to do it in a somewhat different way, by sharing with you my own experience, my own spirituality, my own coming to voice as a black woman, as an African American woman who had to discern the spirits within her and judge whether they were for her liberation or for her further enslavement.

You will notice that I speak first and foremost to my sisters of all races, of all faiths, of all ethnicities who are seeking to survive in today's world but, in so doing, I speak also to all my brothers as well. I seek not to create division but to further understanding, to challenge yet confirm, to encourage all in the struggle toward the true fulfillment of this country's promise as a land of "liberty and justice for all," doing so, hopefully, without alienating you from that same struggle. How can this be done?

How do I, as a black woman whose voice and presence have been marginalized, both because of her race and her sex, in American society and in the Roman Catholic Church--how do I challenge yet affirm? How do I encourage without alienating? How do I, who in many ways have been one of the "least among us," speak to you who in many ways are among the "privileged" in American society today? In trying to come to grips with this mandate, I too have been challenged and also affirmed. I have been forced to retrace some of my own steps along the journey which has brought me to stand before you today.

These are questions, on the level of gender, with which I am sure many of you can identify. You too have been constantly challenged by the institutional structure of our Church which is male, hierarchical, and patriarchal. As white women or as people of color, our presence and participation in the Church has also been challenged and denied. Yet the Church is also an overwhelmingly white structure. That fact must be addressed as well.

I would, therefore, like to share with you just a little of what it means, in Zora Neale Hurston's words, to be "colored [or, in today's understanding, black] me." What does it mean to be an African American Catholic lay theologian in the Church today? What is the value of my witness and the witness of my black sisters and brothers for you?

Coming to Voice

Bell Hooks speaks of the importance of the "coming to voice" of marginalized Third World and African American women today. In *Talking Back*, she quotes a young black woman student:

My voice is not fit to be heard by 120 people. To produce such a voice, my temperature increases and my hands shake. My voice is calm and quiet and soothing; it is not a means of announcing the many secrets my friends have told me--it quiets the rush of the running stream that is their life, slowing to make a mirror to reflect their worries, so that they can be examined and problems rectified. I am not relieved by voicing my opinions. Placing my opinion up to be judged by the public is a form of opening myself to criticism and pain. Those who do not share my eyes cannot see where to tread lightly on me.

I am afraid. I am, and always will be afraid. My fear is that I will not be understood. I try to learn the vocabulary of my friends to ensure my communication on their terms. There is no single vocabulary of 120 people. I will be misunderstood; I will not be respected as a speaker; they will name me Stupid in their minds; they will disregard me. I am afraid.[1]

Her fear in many ways is and has been my own. How do I speak so that others, not of my race or culture, will hear and understand me? How do I speak in ways that affirm my own beliefs, my own experience, but do not threaten or deny at the same time the beliefs, the experience, of others? How do I speak my own language and not that of others and yet be sure that I will be understood?

As a child growing up in Buffalo, New York, I was in many ways the odd one. I was different--everyone agreed on that but they were unsure whether that difference was positive or negative. My parents and sisters loved me in their own way but they did not know quite what to do with me. I taught myself to read when I was three years old and I read anything and everything I could get my hands on--including cereal boxes, advertisements, the classified section of newspapers, anything, because we had little money for books. I was feverishly hungry for knowledge and I swallowed it whole so that when it came time to enter college (a step I always knew I would take), no one, including myself, was sure whether I would major in science (I loved biology and chemistry), history, music (my desire had been to learn every orchestral instrument), languages, or political science.

I began in chemistry at an eastern university where I was one

69

of four newly accepted black students, two male and two female. However, I quickly discovered that the diploma I had earned at my predominantly black high school had not sufficiently prepared me to compete. I began behind most of the other students who, although first-year students like myself, had somehow acquired a more in-depth background by taking courses unavailable to me at East High. It was a terrific shock to my ego and self-esteem to realize that I, who had graduated at the top of my class, was now struggling at the bottom. I left after my freshman year and switched to a language major at the university in my home town, where I could work full time nights and attend classes full time during the days. Eventually, still not fully satisfied, in my senior year I switched to pre-law, with an emphasis in history and political science. I entered law school and eventually began the practice of law in Washington, D.C., where I was the first and only Black to be hired in my division.

My entire experience of education after high school was that of being usually the only Black in my classes as well as one of only a few in the entire department or university. It was challenging, but it was also intimidating. My experience of oppression stemmed from my race more than from my sex, but the latter form was present as well.

The result of constantly being a minority member in my classes was to be a young woman, known at home and around friends for never shutting her mouth, becoming a woman who rarely opened her mouth in class to speak at all, even when directly called upon. Not until the fall of 1979, when I was almost literally knocked off my feet by illness, did I begin to find my voice again. During that time when I, an avid outdoorswoman, was told that a degenerative knee disease might cripple me for life, I became confirmed into the Catholic Church. I had left the African Methodist Episcopal Church at the age of fifteen, denouncing with the righteousness of youth the hypocrisy I felt existed there.

After my confirmation, still unable to walk without assistance, I responded to God's call to study theology. Again, at Catholic University, I was one of only two black women in the department. But the experience was different. Although I was still hesitant

70

about speaking out, I found that I had to. I slowly began to come alive in ways that I did not fully understand. During that eight-year period of theological study in the United States and abroad, I was confronted for the first time with the need to discover who and whose I was. In order to survive, in order to defend my presence in those classes, I had both to name and claim myself, and to hold up my own experience as a valid context out of which to "do theology."

Today, after reading Bell Hooks in preparation for this presentation, I recognize some of what I was experiencing during those crucial years and the importance of the journey that I had begun, a journey, unbeknownst to me, very similar to the journey required of one engaged in the Ignatian Spiritual Exercises. For in that journeying I was enabled to discern the movement of the Spirit within me, to recognize the call of God and haltingly to respond to that call and find my voice--a coming to voice of the inner self that in many ways not only helped me to endure but also freed me so that I could continue the journey. Hooks writes in a powerful way of a similar journeying that many women undergo, stating that:

> . . . for women within oppressed groups who have contained so many feelings--despair, rage, anguish--who do not speak, as poet Audre Lorde writes, "for fear our words will not be heard or welcomed," coming to voice is an act of resistance. Speaking becomes both a way to engage in active self-transformation and a rite of passage where one moves from being object to being subject. Only as subjects can we speak. As objects, we remain voiceless--our beings defined and interpreted by others.[2]

For most of my life, I have been an object--seeing myself only as I was reflected in the eyes of others. I was the odd one, "different" in some way, the one nobody knew quite what to do with. I was a black female yet I did not fit the stereotypes which our society has set forth for black women--ones which, unfortunately, my own culture has too often assimilated. I was neither brazenly promiscuous, nor a mother, nor was I ignorant and dependent. I was always, in many ways, my own woman. I did not know my place. I simply persisted in quietly going my own way, never fully acknowledging the psychic costs, never quite sure where that way was leading me. In many ways, but without recognizing it, I was searching for myself, for my own identity, a step each child must take in order to grow into full maturity but one often denied Blacks and women in American society. As women, we are only allowed to define ourselves as a reflection of our men--fathers, brothers, uncles, husbands, and even sons. As Blacks, we are only allowed to define ourselves in terms of the dominant white structure. I was hemmed in by stereotype, by prejudice, by misunderstanding, a misunderstanding sometimes willful but often earnestly and pain-fully unconscious. I was fighting for my life, to be myself, to define myself, yet consciously aware that my self was different from other selves because of the racism and sexism embedded in our society today.

All too often in that struggle, my greatest challenge came from my own--black men and women or white women--who distrusted my efforts and sought to impede my self-emancipation for reasons of their own. Thus, my struggle was two-sided. It involved the white world, that dominant structure which sought to label and thereby suppress my voice, as well as my own world, that of African Americans, who saw me both as a traitor to the race and to Protestant Christianity because I had dared to be different, even though I had not been aware originally that I was being different. They too attempted to restrain and defeat me and silence my voice.

Finally, after much prayer and discernment--a discernment I might add which is ongoing and neverending--I came to the realization that it was very important for my voice to be heard if only because so many were attempting to stifle it. I recognized, as Mariana Romo-Carmona wrote, that:

Each time a woman begins to speak, a liberating process begins, one that is unavoidable and has powerful political implications.... we see repeated the process of self-discovery, of affirmation in coming out of the closet, the search for a definition of our identity within the family and our community, the search for answers, for meaning in our personal struggles, and the commitment to a political struggle to end all forms of oppression. The stages of increasing awareness become clear when we begin to recount the story of our lives to someone else, someone who has experienced the same changes. When we write or speak about these changes we establish our experiences as valid and real, we begin to analyze, and that analysis gives us the necessary perspective to place our lives in a context where we know what to do next.[3]

We are freed by that analysis, by that coming to self-understanding, to understand that ours is a liberation not just of self but for others, for action in the world on behalf of those unable to act for themselves.

Today I recognize that my words are heard in different ways by different people. They are heard in one way by the oppressor and are often seen as threatening and divisive; they are heard in another way by those engaged with me in the struggle for the liberation of humanity, hopefully as encouraging and affirming.

My voice, I hope, speaks of liberation and challenges those marginalized and invisible in American society of whatever race, sex, or class to uncover, discover, and recover their own voices, to lay claim to and proclaim themselves as subjects of their own history despite the risks that may be involved. I speak in the hope that others will join me, recognizing the fear within but speaking because I, because we, must. With painful consciousness I speak to you today, hoping that you will hear and share in my journeying while you reflect on and share yours with each other.

A Divided History

Writing with a poignancy that betrayed the pain of her own existence, Zora Neale Hurston depicted the condition of African American women with a starkness that, sadly, is still relevant today. She addresses us in the voice of Nanny, the former slavewoman who is speaking to her granddaughter Janie in *Their Eyes Were Watching God:*

> Honey, de white man is de rule of everything as fur as Ah been able tuh find out. Maybe it's some place way off in de ocean where de black man is in power, but we don't know nothin' but what we see. So de white man throw down de load and tell de nigger man tuh pick it up because he have to, but he don't take it. He hand it to his womenfolks. De nigger woman is de mule uh de world so far as Ah can see. Ah been praying fuh it to be different wid you. Lawd, Lawd, Lawd.[4]

73

And so our mothers, our grandmothers, our great-grandmothers and those who came before them have been praying since Blacks were first forcibly introduced to the United States as an enslaved and dehumanized people.

That slavery did not encourage the development of a people but rather thrived upon their degradation. The newly arrived slaves were separated from motherland, family, language, friends--all that was meaningful to them and defined them as a people. Yet, paradoxically, they survived--not completely whole because the devastation was overwhelming, but as a people, they did survive. They managed to retain many aspects of their culture and they nurtured their memories in their music, their prayers, their coming together in what community they were allowed to share.

There has been a great deal of discussion and debate about the impact of slavery on the African American people and whether or not that impact continues to the present day. I will not go into that debate at this time other than to say that one result was the development of a myth which continues to serve to alienate black and white women as well as black women and men to the present day. That is the myth of white womanhood. An integral part of this myth was the polarized depictions of black and white women. White women retained all of the stereotypical positive characteristics--gentle, nurturing, sensitive, intuitive, helpless, dependent-- which served to place white women on a pedestal. Black women were given the negative feminine attributes--temptress, promiscuous, independent, unnatural mother--and were seen as the lowest depths of humanity or, usually, outside of humanity entirely. The black woman was all that a white woman should not be. She was, indeed, the mule of American society, forced to bear burdens the lowest animal was not required to bear and denounced for the very degradation forced upon her. The dichotomy was plain to see. They were women in both groups, as Sojourner Truth pointed out:

> Nobody ever helps me into carriages, or over mud-puddles, or gibs me de best places. And ain't I a woman? Look at me! Look at my arm! I have ploughed, and planted, and gathered into barns, and no man could head me! And ain't I a woman? I could work as much

and eat as much as any man when I could get it, and bear de lash
as well. And ain't I a woman? I have borne thirteen children, and
seen 'em mos' all sold off to slavery, and when I cried out with a
mother's grief, none but Jesus heard me! And ain't I a woman?[5]

Incredibly, however, from this distorted mythology came the
often asserted belief that white women were equally victims of the
oppression of slavery. It was often argued, especially by women
writers who participated in the Abolitionist movement, that the
"physical assaults against black women in slavery; as well as the
psychological deprivation resulting from their lack of control of their
own persons," could be equated "with the white slave mistresses'
psychological pain at their husbands' behavior"[6] in engaging in
sexual activity with their female slaves. Yet, as Linda Brent, herself
a slave, wrote of her white mistress and the issue of slavery:

I was soon convinced that her emotions arose more from anger and
wounded pride. She felt that her marriage vows were desecrated,
her dignity insulted; but she had no compassion for the poor
victims of her husband's perfidy. She pitied herself as a martyr;
but she was incapable of feeling for the condition of shame and
misery in which her unfortunate helpless slaves were placed.[7]

Indeed, rather than being treated with compassion and understanding, the raped slave woman was all too often treated harshly, even
beaten to the point of death, at the order of, and sometimes by, her
enraged and "violated" mistress.

This same bitterness toward the existence of racism still serves
as a barrier to concerted action on the part of feminists of different
races today. The feminist movement, both in society and within the
Church, has been one of white women--usually educated, middle-
class women--with the freedom and privilege to become militant
without fearing consequences as harsh as those to which a woman
of color or lower-class white women would be subjected. In the
Roman Catholic Church, it is especially true that the greater
number of women advocating equality have been religious or lay
women with similar education, freedoms, and privileges. Too often
the experience of white women has been presented as universal,

incorporating and speaking for the experience of all women. It is not that they assume the others are incapable of speaking for themselves; rather, their silence and absence is often not even noted.

As I attempted to show in my brief sharing of my own experience, this silence cannot continue. To attempt to represent others is neither possible nor viable. It leads to the masking of specific differences among women in this country in an effort, albeit unconscious perhaps, to present a united face to one's oppressors. For, as Audre Lorde has noted, "the master's tools will never dismantle the master's house."[8] It is vital that we, as women, uncover and vanquish as best we can the sins of racism and classism that persist in the feminist movement so that we can then work against these evils, as well as the evil of sexism, in our society and in the Church. We must first remove the beam from our own eye before we can attempt to remove the splinter from the eyes of others. We must participate in the struggle for our own redemption even while we are engaged in God's work of redeeming the entire human race.

Many women, of all races, have serious problems with the feminist movement and, therefore, with feminist theology. The image they have received from the media, from Rome, and from other sources is an extremely distorted one, but they are unaware of the distortions. As Hooks notes:

> Many women are reluctant to advocate feminism because they are uncertain about the meaning of the term. Other women from exploited and oppressed ethnic groups dismiss the term because they do not wish to be perceived as supporting a racist movement; feminism is often equated with [the] white women's rights effort. Large numbers of women see feminism as synonymous with lesbianism; their homophobia leads them to reject association with any group identified as pro-lesbian. Some women fear the word "feminism" because they shun identification with any political movement, especially one perceived as radical. [Here I should note that many see feminist theology simply as a radical political group within the Church as well.] Of course there are women who do not wish to be associated with [the] women's rights movement in any form so they reject and oppose [the] feminist movement.[9]

We must recognize that our voices and the experiences that feed them are different. The language used may be the same but the understandings are quite different. This fact can and may lead to confusion at times, but accepting and learning how to work with these differences can and will lead to the emergence of a creative diversity in coalition.

> When feminism is defined in such a way that it calls attention to the diversity of women's social and political reality, it centralizes the experiences of all women, especially the women whose social conditions have been least written about, studied, or changed by political movements. When we cease to focus on the simplistic stance "men are the enemy," we are compelled to examine systems of domination and our role in their maintenance and perpetuation.[10]

There is a problem in the Church today and among its members concerning this issue of diversity. Often I have been confronted by offended whites who accuse me of racism for speaking of a black Catholic spirituality, a black Catholic theology, a black Catholic presence in the Church. They insist that one can only be Catholic. In so doing, they deny the validity of what it means actually to be catholic (with a small "c"). Instead, their claim to catholicity rests in their own self-definition--an ethnocentric definition--which places them at the center and all others on the margin. Their definition fails to reflect truly the diversity of God's creation.

For we are all the People of God; we are all part of God's creation. From the earliest beginnings of the Christian Church, diversity has been upheld as a reflection of the *Imago Dei* (the image of God). All of us, in our various races and ethnicities, reflect God in God's oneness, for God created us as diverse peoples speaking diverse tongues and having diverse cultures. This is all part of God's salvific plan for us. That oneness in God should be seen not as a monolithic oneness but as varied as the sands of the seashore. The constant insistence by one race that there can be only one vision, one expression of Church, is sinful, because it denies the diversity of creation and of the *Imago Dei* and, instead, restricts that image to one race. We must rather, with Ignatius of Loyola, look at the world from the perspective of the blessed Trinity, viewing all of the various peoples on the face of the earth, as he noted, "in such great diversity in dress as in manner of acting. Some are white, some black; some at peace, and some at war; some weeping, some laughing; some well, some sick; some coming into the world, and some dying."[11] But all, all are members of the one human race. We are not all alike nor are we all engaged in the same journey at the same time nor should we be, but we are all creations of the same loving Spirit, placed here to live out our lives as best we can in the freedom granted us all by that same loving Spirit. We were not created the same, but our differences should be a source of constant pleasure, not of continuous division. Insistent emphasis on universality--a universality which is false--is insistence on a lie.

Susan Brooks Thistlewaite, in her insightful book *Sex, Race and God* applies this vision directly to the feminist movement. She asks whether the insistent desire on the part of white women to bond with black women and other women of color "under an undifferentiated label of 'sisterhood'" should be viewed as sin seen as an "inability to respect the boundaries of privacy"[12] of others. I would answer yes to her question. Room must be made for boundaries of cultural and racial differences so that all may have the freedom to explore and develop their own definitions of themselves and thereby grow into full adulthood. Sisterhood is powerful, yes, but only when it is freely offered and freely received, not when it is imposed, too often in a patronizing way, by one race upon another while the imposers continue to live the lie of that "sisterhood" in their own lives and praxis in the world.

Womanist Theology

Black women, in their triple oppression of race, class, and gender, must have the freedom, the space, to empower themselves, to engage in their own efforts at consciousness-raising as well as to share those efforts with others, both male and female. This is now happening with the evolution of the womanist movement, whose strongest voice I see as that of womanist theologians.

A womanist, as Alice Walker defines the term, is a black feminist or feminist of color. She is "wanting to know more and in greater depth than is good for one ... [she is] outrageous, audacious, courageous and [engages in] willful behavior."[13] A womanist is grown and does not mind letting everyone around her know it. A womanist is universal in the sense that her loving includes men and women, sexually and nonsexually, as well as music, dance, food, roundness, the struggle, the Spirit, and herself, "regardless." She is "committed to survival and wholeness of an entire people, male and female" and is opposed to separation, "except for health."[14]

Thus, a womanist sees herself both individually and in community. Her goal of liberation is not simply for herself but for all her people and, beyond that, for all who are also oppressed by reason of race, sex, and class. Sexism is not the only issue for her; rarely is it the most important issue. Rather, the intertwined evils that act to restrict her and her community are cause for her concern. Womanism in many ways can be seen as encompassing feminism in its openness to all who are oppressed. Womanism encompasses all forms of liberation because it seeks what some would identify as the truly ideal: the total liberation of all human beings of every race and nation.

Womanist theologians, therefore, have difficulty with some of the issues raised in both white feminist theology and in black male liberation theology, for both are seen as engaging in "God-talk" from within a too narrowly particular and exclusive context. Both err in seeing their own particular experiences as the norm for all theologizing. Womanist theology insists that full human liberation can only be achieved by the elimination, not of one form of oppression only, but of all forms. Quoting Bell Hooks once again:

As a group, black women are in an unusual position in this society, for not only are we collectively at the bottom of the occupational ladder, but our overall social status is lower than that of any other group....White women and black men have it both ways. They can act as oppressors or be oppressed. Black men may be victimized by racism, but sexism allows them to act as exploiters and oppressors of women. White women may be victimized by sexism, but racism enables them to act as exploiters and oppressors of black people. Both groups have led liberation movements that favor their interests and support the continued oppression of other groups. Black male sexism has undermined struggles to eradicate racism just as white female racism undermines feminist struggle. As long as these two groups or any group defines liberation as gaining social equality with ruling class white men, they have a vested interest in the continued exploitation and oppression of others.[15]

She continues:

Black women with no institutionalized "other" that we may discrimi- nate against, exploit or oppress often have a lived experience that directly challenges the prevailing classist, sexist, racist social structure and its concomitant ideology.[16]

Hooks believes that this experience provides black women with a con- sciousness that enables them to critique the persistent evils still prevalent in our society and, I would add, in our Church, as well as to provide a voice that can enrich the debate on liberation and a praxis that models it.

I am a womanist. Not until I read Walker's definitions and articles by other women of color who have been active in articulating that definition did I truly realize why I had always been uncomfortable when, because of my insistence on studying theology, I was labeled a feminist. I had the same misconceptions that Bell Hooks articulated but was not aware of their content until black women began to name who they were--not, I believe, in opposition to white feminists, but definitely in distinction from them and in hopes of enlarging the understanding of feminism.

Black Catholic Womanist Context

I am, therefore, in basic agreement with Hooks. At the risk of being accused of a parochialism of my own, I would now like to explore briefly the experience of black Catholic women as a source for a womanist theology of liberation.

When we speak of oppression in the Roman Catholic Church, we cannot look simply at the experiences of our white sisters, nor can we look only at the experiences of our black men. Neither is nor can be reflective of what it means to be black, Catholic, and female in the Catholic Church today. When I entered the Catholic Church eleven years ago, I was accused by both family and friends of "turning white." The outward image of our Church is not black or multihued; it is white, an image which denies the history of the Church's origin in the Middle East and in Africa. I had not thought about the racial makeup of the Church when I first entered. My conversion, I believed then and still believe now, was in answer to God's summons. But once I became a Catholic, I quickly was made aware of my "minority" status in many, sometimes unpleasant and painful, ways. This experience triggered a desire in me to learn more about the Church and its earliest beginnings, and I was surprised by what I found.

We do not know our history as Catholics. Unfortunately, what we do know has all too often been bleached beyond recognition. When I speak to audiences--regardless of their racial or ethnic background--of the African fathers of the Church, of the three African popes (Miltiades, Victor, and Gelasius), and of the African martyrs and saints, I am met with surprise, disbelief, and, too often, denial. Often I am indignantly told that those of whom I speak were northern Africans and therefore not black. It is continually amazing to me how a large segment of Africa has managed, historically, to be cut off from that continent and somehow transported to Europe with most interesting results.

But let me not stray from my focus. We all know the importance of consciousness-raising, but we often fail to acknowledge that reflection on self, to be truly valid, must incorporate insights from others unlike ourselves so that we can be privileged to see ourselves as we are mirrored in the eyes of others who are, indeed, "other." Only in this way can we truly discern the spirits within us and their positive or negative influences upon us.

A quiet revolution is brewing within the Catholic Church, one which has gone unnoticed until very recently. Scripture says, "the people that walked in darkness have seen a great light" (Is 9:2). Those people are African American Catholics and, I would argue, most particularly African American Catholic women. As an almost invisible and voiceless people within the Catholic Church, we have had the freedom, in some ways, to "do our own thing." We have been coming to consciousness of ourselves as a people with something of value to offer, not just to ourselves and to other African Americans, not just to the Roman Catholic Church, but to all Christian churches and to the world at large. African American Catholic women and men have been hard at work in the vineyards of the Lord for a long time and the harvest is now coming due.

We are in the process of naming and claiming ourselves, of going back into our history in the Church, and affirming that which we find there. We

81

are excavating the memories of our sojourn in this country, memories often painful but necessary. For we are a people of struggle and "our struggle is also a struggle of memory against forgetting" (South African Freedom Charter). We are also a people of survival and, as part of that survival, we are not ashamed or afraid to name ourselves Catholic.

Over the centuries of our presence in this country and in the Catholic Church, we have, in many ways, been coopted and corrupted into supporting the status quo, into forsaking our own unique identities in our quest to be seen as truly Catholic. But today, African American Catholics are taking their lights out from under the baskets and are letting them shine, shine, shine. They are speaking out on what it means to them to be truly black and authentically Catholic in a holistic, life-affirming and community-building way. They are articulating that meaning for themselves and others in the development of a spirituality and a theology which arise out of the context of their own lived experience in the United States.

Sister Thea Bowman is the example par excellence of black Catholic women today. Any of you who had the privilege of sharing with her recognize her vibrant spirit. I do not know if Thea ever involved herself in a discussion of feminist, womanist, or any other form of liberating theology, but she certainly lived out what they meant in her own life. She was, just as Alice Walker defined, a bold, daring, audacious, courageous woman. She was overwhelming to some but loving and caring to all. She was a black woman and, in all that she said and did, she lived out the meaning of black womanhood. She challenged the status quo, redefined the meaning of Church, and called all within the Church to live up to the gospel message. She theologized in song, in story, in praise of God, in the witness of her life. Sister Thea was a shooting star who flamed through our lives for a brief moment in time and then went home to God. But in that brief time she shared with us she, in her own way, shook the foundations of our world and caused them to tremble, tremble, tremble.

Other bold and daring black Catholic women are taking up Sister Thea's flung banner and holding it aloft for all the world to see. There are only four black Catholic theologians in the United States today, sad testimony to the lingering legacy of racism in the core of our Church. Yet, interestingly enough, three of them are women. They are joined by catechists, liturgists, and administrators of both sexes in proclaiming the voice and spirituality of African American Catholics.

Our spirituality is biblically centered. We do not reject Sacred Scripture but neither do we swallow all of it blindly. Our experience of slavery taught us to read the Bible with black eyes and to proclaim the Word of God with black voices and understanding. We were not moved by the efforts of our masters to implant a biased and distorted Christianity within us; rather, we re-Christianized Christianity, opening it up to its fullest understanding, as a religion of liberation proclaiming a God who created free men and women in God's own image and who gave them a liberator in Christ Jesus, the Son of God.

Our understanding of God and Christ is therefore "colored," if you will, by that liberationist understanding. God and Jesus are not problematic; they are both immanent and transcendent in our lives. The immanent God loves us and nurtures us like a parent bending low over a child yet, as transcendent, God is free to judge those who oppress us and to call us forth into freedom. Jesus as immanent is brother and sister; he is in many ways one of us, walking and talking with us, sharing our journey and carrying our burdens, and suffering the pain of our oppression and rejection. Yet, as transcendent Son of God, he will come forth in glory to lead us to the promised land. We rejoice in the Holy Spirit, that balm of Gilead sent to heal our sin-sick souls, to abide within us and to strengthen us on our journey while giving us the courage to fight back against our oppressors and to "keep on keepin' on." These are the insights we must share. These are the gifts we offer. African American Catholic women have been the bearers and the preservers of our culture, of our heritage, of our faith, and have passed these treasures on to the next generations. They, our foremothers, our "sheroes," through their abiding faith in a God who provides, a God who makes a way out of no way, have given us the courage and the strength to persevere.

As we look at the world today, African Americans realize that, as a people of color, we are not in the minority, nor are we a minority as a people of faith. Nor are we, collectively, as women of all races in the minority. That knowledge is the foundation upon which we must build today. We must look at ourselves, black, white, yellow, red, and brown, and at others, with new eyes reflective of the interconnectedness of our worlds today. Yet, we must also look with eyes reflective of the colorful diversity which makes of us, especially, a catholic people. If we remain blind to each other, we will only continue on our road to ruin. Somehow we must join with our God in working together to ensure the redemption of the human race rather than seeking it for only a chosen few, believed chosen simply because of their race or their class.

To do theology, we must begin within a context. From the particular context of a particular people, all theology develops, whether that fact is recognized or not. We cannot be objective, but we must be aware of and able to articulate our subjectiveness. Today, we must allow the myriad voices of women to ring out in joyous celebration of our diversity and in faith-filled hope of our coming together in a universality which is truly reflective of who and whose we are. Rosemary Radford Ruether writes:

> True universalism must be able to embrace existing pluralism, rather than trying to fit every people into the mould of religion and culture generated from one historical experience. Only God is one and universal. Humanity is finally one because the one God created us all. But the historical mediators of the experience of God remain plural. To impose one religion [or, in our context, one theology or one way of doing theology or of experiencing God] on everyone flattens and impoverishes the wealth of human interaction with God. In order to be truly catholic, Christians must revise the imperialistic way they have defined their universality.[17]

The situation in the Catholic Church is fraught with problems. We are challenged to be more than we are, for we are called to recognize our own vocation in Christ Jesus, the liberator of all humanity. We are called to do the work of God in bringing about a kingdom of truth and justice. Yet to do so, to be free to heed that call, we must be freed from the power of sin, perhaps personal in nature but nevertheless cultural and social in its pervasive and negative impact.

We can react to the oppression, whether of race, class, or sex, simply by leaving the Church in frustrated anger and pain; or we can remain and continue to serve as a "thorn" in its side, remembering that the institutional structure is well and truly man-made but that we are the Church as the People of God. That has been my choice. We can also make the sad mistake of those who seek not to change the structures themselves but only their outward manifestation, resulting in empowerment for only a few, a few more black priests and bishops, a few, in time, woman priests, but leaving the hierarchical, authoritarian entity intact. Or we can work to restructure, from within, our Church and make it truly ours. We can do this work as individuals, Blacks working for Black liberation, Hispanics for Hispanic liberation, native Americans, Asians, white women, black men; or we can choose to work together, recognizing and rejoicing in our differences while finding solidarity in our mutual struggle and shared faith. We must, in all reality, learn to survive together or surely we will be destroyed one by one. I can think of no greater model of survival than black Catholic women who have fought on all sides to retain their faith and to pass it on.

Listen to Audre Lorde:

> As women, we have been taught either to ignore our differences, or to view them as causes for separation and suspicion rather than as forces for change. Without community there is no liberation, only the most vulnerable and temporary armistice between an individual and her oppression. But community must not mean a shedding of our difference, nor the pathetic pretense that these differences do not exist.
>
> Those of us who stand outside the circle of this society's definition of acceptable women; those of us who have been forged in the crucibles of difference--those of us who are poor, who are lesbians, who are Black, who are older--know that survival is not an academic skill.
>
> It is learning how to stand alone, unpopular and sometimes reviled, and how to make common cause with those others identified as outside the structures in order to define and seek a world in which we can all flourish. It is learning how to take our differences and make them our strengths. For the master's tools will never dismantle the master's house. They may allow us temporarily to beat him at his own game, but they will never enable us to bring about genuine change. And this fact is only threatening to those women who still define the master's house as their only source of support.[18]

In this setting, the setting of a university, a Catholic university, we have the freedom to stretch our minds, both as teacher and as student, to lay bare the meaningful questions that challenge our existence. We can stifle that inquiry by allowing our minds to grow dull and uninquisitive, refusing to challenge or be challenged; or we can open the doors to critical ideas, ideas that may shake the foundations of our very existence but that will also prevent us from growing complacent. This challenge I give to all of you, regardless of race or class or sex. By sharing with you my own experience and that of black women, I challenge you to learn from each other, to share with each other, to grow with each other. My expression of love for you, my white sisters and brothers, is to call you to account for the racism and sexism that lurks insidiously within your midst and to denounce it for the demon that it is, so that we may come together without barriers and truly be about the work of the kingdom. My expression of love for my sisters and brothers of color is to recognize and name the anger and pain that is within us and to work as well to destroy the sexism and racism within our own midst, so that we can truly walk together with the Lord.

I leave you with a poem that I have carried around with me for years while I struggled to understand who I was and where God was leading me. It is the words of a mother to her son, but it has always spoken powerfully to me, a daughter. It is in many ways a poem about my own mother who has "been through the storm" but never looked back, for her eyes were always watching God. The poem, by Langston Hughes, is entitled

Mother to Son

Well, son, I'll tell you:
Life for me ain't been no crystal stair.
It's had tacks in it,
and splinters,
and boards torn up,
and places with no carpet on the floor
Bare.
But all the time
I'se been a-climbin' on,
And reachin' landin's,
And turnin' corners,
And sometimes goin' in the dark
Where there ain't been no light,
So, Boy, don't you turn back.
Don't you set down on the steps
'Cause you finds it's kinder hard.
Don't you fall now--
For I'se still goin', honey,
I'se still climbin',
and life for me ain't been no crystal stair.[19]

Notes

[1] Bell Hooks, *Talking Back: Thinking Feminist, Thinking Black* (Boston: South End Press, 1989), 17.

[2] Ibid., 12.

[3] Ibid.

[4] Zora Neale Hurston, *Their Eyes Were Watching God* (New York: Harper and Row, 1990), orig. publ. 1937, 29.

[5] See Bell Hooks, *Ain't I a Woman? Black Women and Feminism* (Boston: South End Press, 1981), 160.

[6] Susan Brooks Thistlethwaite, *Sex, Race, and God: Christian Feminism in Black and White* (New York: Crossroad, 1989), 33.

[7] See Hooks, *Ain't I a Woman?*, 28.

[8] Audre Lorde, *Sister Outsider: Essays and Speeches* (Freedom, Calif.: The Crossing Press, 1984), 112.

[9] Bell Hooks, *Feminist Theory: From Margin to Center* (Boston: South End Press, 1984), 23.

[10] Ibid., 25.

[11] *The Spiritual Exercises of St. Ignatius*, trans. Louis J. Puhl, S.J. (Chicago: Loyola University Press, 1951), 50.

[12] Thistlethwaite, op. cit., 86.

[13] Alice Walker, *In Search of Our Mothers' Gardens: Womanist Prose* (New York: Harcourt Brace Jovanovich, 1983), xi.

[14] Ibid.

[15] *Feminist Theory*, 14-15.

[16] Ibid., 15.

[17] Rosemary Ruether, *To Change the World: Christology and Cultural Pluralism* (New York: Crossroad, 1981), 39.

[18] *Sister Outsider*, 112.

[19] Langston Hughes, *Selected Poems of Langston Hughes* (New York: Alfred Knopf, 1977), 187. (With permission.)

George W. Hunt, S.J.

Jesuit Journalism: Between the Trenches and the Ivory Tower

George W. Hunt, S.J. is President and Editor in Chief of America Publications.

I t is a great pleasure for me to return to Georgetown University where I have very, very happy memories. Let me begin by saying, as all of you know by watching movies and television and perhaps from working on newspapers yourselves, editors always demand of reporters that all stories answer the questions, Who? What? When? Where? Why? As an editor myself, I suppose I should put such advice into practice, because I will be recounting fragments of the story of Jesuit journalism in this country, specifically the story of *America* magazine, our Jesuit journal. Consequently, I will shape my remarks around these five questions: Who, What, Where, When, Why. But I will shift the order around a bit and postpone the Who question and link it up later with the Why question, because the Who and Why questions together address the central theme of this Georgetown University lecture series. So let me begin.

What is *America* and when does it appear and where? Each of these questions can be answered in a few short sentences. First, *America* is a weekly Catholic magazine, in fact, the only weekly Catholic magazine in the United States, and it is edited and published by the Jesuits. Unlike more popular magazines or glossies like *Time* and *Newsweek* and *People*, it is a journal of opinion. *America* offers to an educated general readership a reasonably coherent analysis of the current events of the day along with editorial proposals and criticisms. It includes wide-ranging articles on sundry subjects that reflect the individual author's own personal analysis and judgment. As for the Where, *America* is composed and published in midtown Manhattan, and it is printed in a firm close by the Cincinnati airport. From there it is mailed to the edges of our country and to the ends of the earth. We reckon that, on the conservative side, at least sixty thousand people and probably many more read the magazine each week.

The When question inevitably touches upon the origins of *America*, and to answer that question demands not only longer sentences but some storytelling. That story in turn is important because it implicitly answers all the other questions, especially the Who and the Why questions which I have saved for last. The story of *America* from its founding up to 1991 coincides with the cultural rhythms, blind spots and visions, bellicose and pacific instincts of the American society and of the Catholic Church throughout the century.

America published its first issue on April 17, 1909, eighty-two years ago; but that date was actually more of a climax than a commencement. To appreciate it one must recall that, once upon a time a century ago, Americans lived in an era when the press was all-powerful; Joseph Pulitzer and William Randolph Hearst bestrode the world like colossi, while their charges not only reported on wars and other conflagrations, but sometimes effectively began them, as in the Spanish-American War in 1898. The daily newspapers and weeklies were the primary shapers and distorters of public opinion, while the over fifty nationally known monthly magazines like *Ladies Home Companion* (which actually had over a million subscribers in 1900), *Collier's*, *Cosmopolitan*, and others dramatically influenced American tastes and culture. This was the era when the caution "Don't believe everything you read in the papers" was very popular precisely because of the fact that most people did. They simply had no other option.

A corollary to this credulity was that they also believed that, if something did not appear in print, it was unimportant. This tendency created an unhappy situation for the Catholic Church at the time. The major newspapers and monthlies were, in the main, published and edited by WASPs, who were either indifferent or hostile to Catholicism, and, if not either, were blithely ignorant of it. To them Catholicism was as foreign, backward, ignorant, and pugnacious a religion as were the Catholics they encountered. And the number of those Catholics was growing alarmingly. The period from 1890 to 1915 was the greatest age of immigration into the United States in our history. And the majority were Catholics from eastern, central and southern Europe, who like their fellow Jews on board the ships of passage were abjectly poor. Church officials and priests and nuns and laity expended all their energies to assimilate these continual hoards of newcomers, to provide them with at least a grade school education, to build them churches, to care for their health, to strengthen their families and, most of all, to offer their children hope.

Meanwhile, and more than coincidentally, anti-Catholic big-otry once again raised its ugly head. Shortly before the Civil War, because of the influx of so many Irish Catholics, the Know-Nothing Nativist Party and associated secret groups rallied and railed against what they called popery and foreign influences and sought to elect only native-born Americans to office, thereby excluding those newly arrived Irish. During the Civil War and its aftermath, such public bigotry against Catholics went into a brief remission. But by the 1890s, the arrival of armies of Catholics--Italians, Poles, Croatians, Slovaks, Austrians, Southern Germans--all of whom appeared even more foreign than the Irish once had, resurrected these various versions of anti-Catholic nativism. These sentiments inspired widely read literature, many hate pamphlets, and innumerable newspapers and magazines. The insinuation bubbling beneath the loathing was this question: How could these ignorant, priest-ridden masses ever be expected to become loyal Americans, citizens who respected our Constitution and our Bill of Rights, people who voted and thought for themselves and did not think the pope's thoughts or their priests' thoughts, people who could become like us, participate in our culture, and share in our national life? Well, the answer was evident: not very likely, in fact, impossible. This, then, was the historical context toward the end of the nineteenth century when the Jesuits began their discussions about the possibility of publishing a journal.[1]

In 1865, right here at Georgetown, Jesuits had begun publish-ing a monthly called *The Messenger of the Sacred Heart*. This magazine encouraged Catholic devotions primarily and addressed an audi-ence less well educated and less interested in controversial matters of church and state. Nonetheless, perhaps owing to this very limitation, *The Messenger of the Sacred Heart* soon became immensely successful and counted over eighty thousand subscribers in 1900 alone--and it lasted, by the way, into the 1970s. Still, despite these numbers of subscribers, the Jesuits guessed and rightly guessed that this readership would not be converted easily into enjoying intellectually demanding or less than spiritually heartening articles. The question was what to do.

First, the Jesuits considered publishing a monthly scholarly magazine, composed by learned Jesuits here and abroad, that would consist of lengthy articles addressing current controversies. Their model for such a monthly derived from recent Jesuit efforts in Europe, all of which postdate the Civil War: *Civilta Cattolica* in Italy, *Etudes* in France, *The Month* in Ireland, and *Stimmen der Zeit* in Germany. The discussants were enthusiastic about the project. Within a short time a staff was chosen, length and format determined, and all systems were on go as they awaited the approval of their superior general in Rome. But this magazine died aborning. Two reasons stand out.[2] First, the rector of Woodstock College (the Jesuit theologate in Maryland), had grave reservations and expressed them often by letter to the Jesuit General and other influential people in Rome. He had reservations about the personalities involved, specifically, about the provincial of the then New York-Maryland Province, Father Thomas Campbell. In the rector's opinion, Campbell was keen on the new magazine, as he was keen on a lot of things, but he had not been careful enough about the "risks" involved. The rector also had misgivings about the prospective editor, Father Ralph Dewey, a young Jesuit noted for his high-handedness and obstinacy.[3]

The second reason was the lack of Jesuit talent and Jesuit manpower. As one of the other provincial superiors put it while this discussion was going on, he was against the idea "because of our incapacity intellectually and our dearth of men." Now this remark is not quite as slighting as it sounds, when one considers that, in less than seven decades after the restoration of the Society, the Jesuits had been stretching their scanty personnel resources and had founded schools, colleges, parishes, and missions in nearly every state in the union. Most of them still thrive.

(I should not end this particular section on a blue note. The Jesuit provincial, Father Thomas Campbell, even out of office was very supportive of Jesuit journalism and became the second editor of *America* magazine in 1910. As for the idea of having a scholarly monthly, *America* began to publish one in 1928 that eventually became a quarterly. It still exists as *Thought*, the Fordham University quarterly. But back to our story.)

Over a decade later, hopes for a Jesuit journal were renewed when the right man and the right hour coincided. That man was the Jesuit John Wynne, a New Yorker born in 1859 and one of the most remarkable figures in American Catholic history. Not only was he founder of *America* magazine; he was also the editor and coordinator of the *Catholic Encyclopedia*, a monumental task for that age and any age. He was responsible for the first translation of the Latin Missal into English. He was the promoter of the cause of the North American Martyrs--Saint Isaac Jogues, John de Brebeuf, and their companions--as well as the author of numerous books. He was brilliant, imaginative, even robust (he lived to be ninety years old). Not unlike so many exceptional people, Wynne did not suffer fools gladly, perhaps because these very people often misunderstood him badly, deeming him too secular or not Catholic enough or possessed of "too many ideas." Most remarkable, though, was his achievement at *America*. His vision for the magazine perdures; the style, the shape, the audience, and the purposes he articulated continue essentially unchanged these many years. In so many ways *America* remains Wynne's little paper, which is what both his admirers and his detractors called it back in 1909.

In 1891 at the age of thirty-two, Father Wynne became the editor of *The Messenger of the Sacred Heart*. That monthly magazine which, as I mentioned, was essentially the publishing arm of the Apostleship of Prayer, grew in circulation and prestige under his leadership; nonetheless, Wynne himself began to grow disenchanted with the magazine's limited horizons. He felt it did not meet the needs of those many Catholics whose concerns were not restricted to devotional subjects. As a result, on his own in May 1900 he drew up a sixteen-page proposal for publishing a new Jesuit periodical which he submitted to his superiors in the New York-Maryland Province.

In the proposal Wynne articulated the kind of review he had in mind and the reasons for it. First, he said, the new periodical would treat "questions of the day and theology, philosophy, ethics, science, literature, history, current as well as past history, art, including drama and music, and giving important news to Catholics." Second, the magazine, he argued, was necessary to "save our people from error," because, he noted, not only were nearly half of

American Catholics then taught in public schools, but most attended non-Catholic colleges, and the newspapers they read contained many errors about Catholicism. Furthermore, he stressed that "our business and professional men live in a Protestant or infidel or irreligious atmosphere."⁴ The third reason he gave was that contemporary Catholic magazines were too limited in scope and audience. The more popular ones--like *Ave Maria, The Rosary, The Messenger of the Sacred Heart*--he said were "too limited to pious subjects, or, by their very names appealed to pious readers only."⁵

Wynne candidly admitted that *The Messenger of the Sacred Heart* itself had become schizophrenic. Of late he and his staff had been forced to publish nondevotional articles on subjects like divorce, biblical criticism, the utilitarians, and the labor problem with the result that, as he candidly put it, it is "edited partly as a high class religious magazine for the more intelligent among the laity and partly as an organ of the Apostleship of Prayer, and it is not therefore effecting either purpose successfully."⁶ Wynne proposed a high-class, thoroughly Catholic organ to instruct Catholics in their faith and combat the intense nationalism of that day by reminding them that they were members of a universal, transnational Church. He added that he preferred a weekly rather than a monthly, along the lines of the weekly London *Tablet*, which had been established about fifty years before. He proposed a starting date in 1902. Once again, Jesuit superiors did not seem keen on the idea and nothing happened from their end.

Undeterred as always, Wynne followed his own lights and in 1902 started two new magazines on his own. The first he called *The Catholic Mind*, which would reprint selected scholarly articles culled from Catholic and usually Jesuit magazines throughout the world. He would translate them, of course, and they would be printed every two weeks and, later each month, in 16- to 32-page editions. Wynne began *The Catholic Mind* "as an experiment." The experiment lasted for another eighty years until in 1982 the xerox machine and other reproduction mechanics effected its demise.

The second magazine grew out of Wynne's decision to split *The Messenger of the Sacred Heart* into two monthly magazines. One would remain the devotional organ of the Apostleship of Prayer and retain its original name. The second he would simply call *The Messenger*, and it was to be a Catholic magazine of general interest. This second magazine, *The Messenger*, not only became a natural parent for its offspring, *America*, but, more to the point, its success convinced doubters at the time, especially Jesuit superiors, about the need for and effectiveness of such a journal. Wynne lost no time in using the instrumentality of his new *Messenger*. By the end of 1902 he himself had become nationally famous.

His fame derived from two long series of articles he wrote in *The Messenger*. The first, entitled "Poisoning the Wells," was an attack on the recently published *Appleton's Universal Cyclopedia and Atlas*. The atlas included several articles on religion that Wynne felt defamed Catholicism. He reprinted his articles in a pamphlet--they actually sold over seventy-five thousand copies at the time--and encouraged Catholics to boycott the Appleton Publishing Company. His strategy worked. Wynne received, and subsequently published, a personal apology from Mr. Appleton himself and a promise to revise the anti-Catholic material. This episode was significant, in fact a historical turning point. Father Wynne was the first to organize and arouse Catholics' sentiment against the prevailing anti-Catholic bigotry via the mails alone, not by direct face-to-face relations. Others, of course, were inspired by his example.[7]

A second series of articles, entitled "The Friars Must Stay," became equally famous. These articles were a defense of those Spanish religious, mostly Franciscan priests in the Philippines, who were to have their lands confiscated and themselves expelled because of the antipathy of the Filipino revolutionaries and the complicity of American representatives there following the Spanish-American War. Wynne saw anti-Catholic bigotry here at work once again as indicative of American foreign policy and domestic policy, and so he sent his article to President Theodore Roosevelt. President Roosevelt was genuinely impressed by his arguments and encouraged Wynne to publish and distribute them "on a large scale so that the whole country might know that there is another opinion on this subject than that which had heretofore prevailed."[8] Thereafter, until Theodore Roosevelt died, he and Wynne remained very cordial friends. These and other polemical successes on Wynne's part demonstrated the value of an articulate, intelligent journal of opinion, even to what we might call the untruest of believers.

Fortunately, in 1907, the Jesuits elected a new superior general, Franz Xavier Ernst, who was foresighted about the importance of journalism as an apostolate (he is the one who encouraged *Razón e Fe* and other journals in Europe). He was very enthusiastic about what he saw in Wynne's *Messenger* and wrote to him about this. Thus encouraged, Wynne prepared a questionnaire for provincial superiors and selected Jesuits throughout the United States to sound out their sentiments about replacing his *Messenger* with "a review," as he called it then. The questions that he posed to them were, like him, most practical. First, should "Catholic" be part of the magazine's name? Second, should it be a weekly or a monthly? Third, what topics or kinds of articles should be included or excluded?

Upon receiving the results of the questionnaire, Wynne came to several conclusions. First, the magazine would be a weekly review of events and questions of the day affecting religion and morality. Second, it would contain short articles of timely interest, since, as he realized, "readers in the United States and Canada, and it seems true of readers everywhere, do not read long or serious articles but prefer accurate information as soon as possible and in briefest form."[9] Third, the articles would treat the broadest range of subjects that might be of interest to contemporary readers.

Thus armed, Wynne undertook a rather extraordinary journey by transportation standards of that era. He visited Jesuit houses throughout the country, first New England, then Maryland, on to Cleveland, Detroit, Chicago. He stopped in as far as Denver and Spokane and Seattle, travelled down the coast to Santa Clara, San Francisco, Los Angeles, and then swung south to New Orleans. His intention was to drum up the enthusiasm of his fellow Jesuits, recruit contributors and staff, and hear their suggestions. He found to his delight that Jesuit enthusiasm in the ranks was genuine and widespread, and it likely aided Wynne in refining his ideas about the new magazine.

He wrote that "laymen prominent in their professions, law,

education, science"[10] should be invited to write for this review, and he described the prospective audience as "Catholic men and women who have had the advantage of higher education, also men of affairs, professional men, libraries, and a fair number of non-Catholics." In a later memorandum Wynne wrote that Catholics need--it is remarkable how farsighted a man he was--"to distinguish clearly between what is of faith and obligatory in practice and what is only a pious belief or devotion."[11] He said that in politics Catholics need "guidance to take their part in the national life and in public affairs and in social movements," rather than stand aloof as they had been doing. As for education, Wynne felt Catholics "should not antagonize the public system but help to make it as good a working one as possible"--quite different from the way others felt at the time. Finally, he expressed the hope that Catholics now might "create or arouse or foster a Catholic sentiment regarding literature and the arts and the social sciences that will gradually extend to non-Catholics, and influence in some measure the literature, the art, and the politics of our national life."

After his travels and after his thought, by 1909 everything was more or less agreed upon, save for one major decision: what should they name the magazine? Here the decisions are most revealing. Wynne himself preferred the name *The Freeman*. These were the reasons he offered: first, *"Freeman"* as a title best reflected the historical legacy of the Jesuits. As he himself wrote, the Society of Jesus was chiefly the instrument of Divine Providence to help men know they were free agents. *The Spiritual Exercises of St. Ignatius* are themselves instructions on "the right use of freedom, and the Jesuit mission in the world has been to promote true liberty and the proper use of it."[12] Second, he said, *Freeman* also best reflects the American experience of liberty. As he put it, "the name *Freeman* expresses perfectly the one object for which it seems to me we should publish the review: namely, to enable Catholic citizens to take their part in public affairs and to mix with their non-Catholic associates."

The provincials, however, rejected the name *The Freeman*. The reason was a good one, I think. They rejected it because of its potential association in people's minds with a racist, intemperate publication called *The Freeman's Journal* that had been published by an arch-conservative Catholic convert just a few decades before. Other proposed names were *The Truth, Old and New, Word and Work*--the last two were especially popular. The voting was split and indecisive, so the decisive Father Wynne himself chose the name *America*, a name suggested by Father Thomas Gannon, who was then the rector of the Jesuit Novitiate at St. Andrews on the Hudson in Poughkeepsie, New York, and a former provincial. Gannon's original suggestion was *Amerika* with a "k"--it reminds you of the 1960s. Wynne thought *"America"* sounded good but found the "k" to be a bit pretentious. So he dropped the "k" and kept the "c."

Interestingly enough, many bishops and priests throughout the country had strongly recommended that the word "Catholic" be omitted from the title page. A compromise was reached by calling the new journal *America* with a subtitle "A Catholic Review of the Week."

The first issue of *America* appeared April 17, 1909, and Father Wynne himself wrote the editorial announcement describing the aims and intents of the new magazine. This rather lengthy announcement is, in fact, a publicly rendered distillation of the goals and themes that required those two decades of discussion and reflection and testing. Listen to the way in which Wynne himself summarizes it: he writes that *America*'s purpose is "to meet the needs of the time," and goes on to list those needs right away:

> A review and conscientious criticism of the life and literature of our day, a discussion of actual questions and the study of vital problems from the Christian standpoint [notice he does not say Catholic, he says Christian deliberately], a record of religious progress, a defense of sound doctrine, an authoritative statement of the position of the Church in the thought and the activity of modern life, a removal of traditional prejudice, a refutation of erroneous news, and a correction of misstatements about belief and practices which millions hold dearer than life.[13]

The somewhat sectarian sound of those phrases is softened immediately by this more ecumenical statement:

> Owing to the wide scope of its contents and its strict avoidance of

proselytism and of all unnecessary criticism, it is hoped that this review will prove attractive, not only to Catholics, but also to the large number of non-Catholics who desire information about Catholic affairs.

These were his broader aims. What were the programs? Here Wynne is quite pithy. He states that *America* intends to:

Discuss questions of the day affecting religion, morality, science and literature, give information and suggest principles that may help to solve vital problems constantly thrown upon our people [meaning the American people], and these discussions will not be speculative or academic, but practical and actual [the word *actual* at that time meant *immediate*], with the invariable purpose of meeting some immediate need of truth, of creating interest in some social work or movement, of developing sound sentiment, and of exercising proper influence in public opinion.

He ended by saying "*America* will strive to broaden the scope of Catholic journalism and become a bond of union among Catholics and a factor in social and civil life."

With the foregoing historical narrative I have answered the When question. The When answer, which is the story of *America*'s start, capsulates the Who and the Why questions. The Who remain the same. The editors are Jesuits as are the majority of our contributors, joined, as Father Wynne hoped, by outstanding lay Catholics and non-Catholics, as well as bishops and priests and nuns. The Who of our readership also remains the same, and so do their expectations. In a recent survey that we conducted, we asked our readers, "Why do you read *America*?" The overwhelming majority gave as their principle reason "to keep informed on Catholic views of contemporary issues," while twenty percent said "because it is an intelligently informed Catholic magazine." The remaining seventeen percent said they trust the magazine "to present an objective, balanced coverage of events."

Father Wynne, I think, would be as heartened by that survey as we were. These are the reasons why our readers read *America*, but, you might ask, Why do Jesuits continue to edit it, with so many other pressing needs, obvious needs in education--and this is why I mention the "ivory tower"--and needs among the poor and

101

helpless throughout the world--"the trenches"? Why do Jesuits assign some of their most talented men to popular journalism, to a fate somewhere between the trenches and the ivory tower?

Allow me to address this crucial Why question with some brief concluding remarks. First, as Jesuit Avery Dulles pointed out in a famous essay, the basic reality on which the Church is founded is a mystery of communication: the Word was made flesh and dwelt among us.[14] Jesus the medium literally is the message. He is the Word of God who has communicated to us what God is like. Jesus communicated through parable and aphorism, stories, symbolic action. Furthermore, all the familiar terms that we use in Christianity are terms of communication. The Bible simply means "the Book," and Christians and Jews are "people of the Book." The basic content of Christian faith rests on the gospel, meaning the good news, and the *kerygma*, the verbal proclamation of that news. Apostles were those commissioned to witness, to communicate the news, while prophets were those who spoke in the name of God. The Church, or the *ecclesia*, were composed of those "called to-gether," those inspired by men and women of the Word. The very purpose of the Church was to bring people into communion, to enable them to communicate with each other and with God. One might say, as Avery Dulles suggests, that today the Church aspires to be a vast international communications network, heeding God's voice in the events of our personal and public history. *America* feels that it is but one more instrument in this Church enterprise.

Second, more specifically connected with the themes of this series, the Jesuit order was founded four hundred fifty-one years ago to be of service to the Church. The word *service* was the one most frequently used by Ignatius himself to describe the Society's mission. Central to that mission of service was the need for what Ignatius termed the "discernment of spirits," the effort aided by grace to determine the proper course of action or the correct order of priorities when one encounters conflicting passions or pressures. Ignatius restricted his analysis of discernment to the interior life of the individual; but, by analogy, his recommendations can be applied to the public arena of contemporary conflict. The great document of Vatican II, the Constitution on the Church in the

Modern World, *Gaudium et Spes*, boldly states that "the Church has always had the duty of scrutinizing the signs of the times and of interpreting them in the light of the gospel."[15] We think that this is precisely the task of *America* each week. Scrutiny of the signs of the times, discernment, and then interpretation in the light of the gospel, these three characterize the efforts of Jesuit journalists.

Unfortunately, we all live in a desensitized world where such efforts are unpopular and often onerous, where the word *conscience*, which is historically a moral category, has been transformed into a psychological category equivalent to a sense of well-being or having-it-altogether, so we at *America* attempt to sensitize or perhaps resensitize the consciences of our readers, not so much to form consciences, but rather to inform our readers so that they too might scrutinize, discern, interpret, discover their own consciences.

Finally, there are two pivotal meditations in the handbook called *The Spiritual Exercises of St. Ignatius* that I think really animate the hearts of all Jesuit journalists. The first is the meditation on the Incarnation in the second week of the Exercises, in which Ignatius invites the retreatant to imagine the following from the perspective of God. He writes:

> See all those people on the face of the earth, and such great variety of dress and ways of acting; some are white, some black, some at peace, some at war, some weeping, some laughing, some well, some sick, some coming to birth, some dying. Then listen to what they are saying, how they speak to each other, how they swear and blaspheme.

This is the world on which Ignatius is obviously inviting us to reflect, to which Christ will come, and to which we believe he continues to come in 1991. It is a world of endless diversity, a world of moral contrasts, a world worth listening to, and a world worth redeeming.

In the second meditation, entitled "The contemplation for achieving divine love," Ignatius invites the person at prayer to:

> Reflect how God dwells in creatures in the elements, giving them existence, and the plants, giving them life, and the animals, conferring upon them sensation, in humans, bestowing understanding. So God dwells in me and gives me personal existence, life, sensation, intelli-

gence, and makes a temple of me since I am created in the likeness and image of the divine majesty.

These two meditations, these two perspectives, answer best, I think, that Why question about *America* and the Jesuit apostolate in journalism.

Notes

[1] This historical overview is a personal distillation of several fine histories of this period. See James Hennesey, *American Catholics* (New York: Oxford University Press, 1981); Philip Gleason, *Keeping the Faith* (Notre Dame: University of Notre Dame Press, 1987); Gerald Fogarty, *The Vatican and the American Hierarchy* (Stuttgart: Hiersemann, 1982); Jay Dolan, *The American Catholic Experience* (Garden City, N.Y.: Doubleday, 1985).

[2] Throughout, I am indebted to Father John L. Ciani and his excellent unpublished Master's thesis for his close historical study of this period. See John L. Ciani, "Sufficiently Indicated in Its Name: The Founding of *America* Magazine and the Development of American Catholic Identity" (Weston School of Theology, 1987). His study is supplemented on occasion by Thurston S. Davis, "What is 'America'?" in *America* (11 April 1959), 92-103; and Francis X. Talbot's biography, *Richard Francis Tierney* (New York: America Press, 1930).

[3] Ibid., 14-22.

[4] Ibid., 44.

[5] Ibid., 45.

[6] Ibid.

[7] Ibid., 46-51.

[8] Ibid., 52.

[9] Ibid., 70.

[10] Ibid., 71.

[11] Ibid., 75.

[12] Ibid., 79.

[13] John L. Ciani, *America*, 17 April 1989 announcement, 5.

[14] Avery Dulles, "The Church Is Communications," *The Catholic Mind* (October 1971), 6-16.

[15] *Gaudium et Spes*, "The Church in the Modern World," paragraph 4 in Walter M. Abbott, ed., *The Documents of Vatican II* (New York: Crossroad, 1989), 201-2.